A Guide to NOT Being Bad

How to NOT be a complete Jackass

Riders on the Rim

The INTRODUCTION could be here but instead it's in the back of the book: (P134) you don't care why I wrote the book, YOU just want to read it. Go ahead. Catch you later . . .

THE BAD DRIVER'S HANDBOOK
A Guide to Being Bad

iUniverse books may be ordered through booksellers or by contacting:

iUniverse LLC
1663 Liberty Drive
Bloomington, IN 47403
www.iuniverse.com
1-800-Authors (1-800-288-4677)

ISBN: 978-1-4917-1080-7 (sc)
ISBN: 978-1-4917-1081-4 (e)

Printed in the United States of America.

iUniverse rev. date: 10/21/2013

BAD DRIVERS HANDBOOK INDEX

Intro, Riders 1
Copyright 2
Index 3
Hey Detroit.................... 4
Toes, Perfect, Slow 5
Questionnaire 6,7
Psych Profile 8, 9, 10
Hell Driver, Right 11
Laser Meter 12
No Ticket, Hints 13
Late excuses,Test 14
Right of Way 15, 16
Speed limits, Faster...... 17
Chatter.......................... 18
Bumper Stickers........... 19
Segways, Scooters,
Cycles, Coopers 20
Hummers,18 wheelers,
No headlights 21
Hitchhikers, STOP, Speed
limits, Traffic................ 22
Exam 23, 24, 25, 26, 27
Lies, BlueDevil............ 28
Ticket, 4Way 29
No Arrest, Wha?........... 30
Evel, Laptop, Al........... 31
Ten Reasons 32
WTF 33
WTF. 2,Quotes............. 34
Pledges 35
King of the Road 36
Queen of the Road...... 37
Potpourri 38
Turret........................... 39
Flatliners, Cougar 40
NoNo's...................... 41
Salesman 42
Fire 43
More Bumpers 44
Misteakes 45
Jail.............................. 46
Driver-nitions.............. 47
What If? 1,2 .... 48, 49

Female Profile............ 50
Male Profile................ 51
What If? 3,4 .... 52, 23
Prince 54
States........................... 55
Baddest driver 56
CARmelita 57
It's not fair................... 58
Rite of Way, Fame........ 59
Tickets......................... 60
Hall of Shame 61
Big City....................... 62
Joy Ride, City............. 63
More City Rulz 64
Test.............................. 65
Jeopardy 66
Jeopardy, too 67
Fast & Furious........ 68, 69
More Fast 70, 71
Dickionary................... 72
DON'T 73, 74
Bad Idea Fil................ 75
Bad Machine............... 76
Look What If? 5 77
RudeRulz..................... 78
RudeRules.Too............ 79
Return What If? 6........ 80
WANTED.................... 81
Donuts 82
Eye Chart................... 83
Rev.What If? 7 84
What If? 8 85
Cop Chasing................ 86
SuperBAD.................. 87
Jail, Los? 88
Evaluation 89
Mumbles 90
MoreMumbles............. 91
Stickers....................... 92
Road Songs 93
Lyin' Cage.................. 94
Lyin' Cage 2 95
Lyin' Cage 3 96
Lyin' Cage 4 97

Bad Driving Signs 98
Bad Signs Too 99
Prevaricators Cage 100
Dreaded What If 9...... 101
What If? 10 102
Hole Truth 103
Hole Truth Too 104
Car Talk...................... 105
Books......................... 106
Books?...................... 107
More Car Talk 108
What If? 11................. 109
What If Even 12......... 110
Believe It 111
Daffynitions 112
Bumper Snickers........ 113
Stupid Quiz 114
More Stupid 115
Excuses 116
More Excuses............. 117
Problems,12 ways 118
What If. 13 119
Holy What If 14 120
Stupid, Matt,Text 121
Fill Blanks................. 122
Road Rage, Tricks...... 123
More Snickers 124
Its Their Fault............. 125
10 reasons, Ticket....... 126
5Toons 127
Final Quotes 128
Sayings...................... 129
Last What If? 15........ 130
Satan,Viper 131
King What If? 16....... 132
Guarantees.................. 133
Intro........................... 134
Afterward 135
Questionnaire 136
Questionnaire2 137
Autograph Page.......... 138

Bother celebrities,
Annoy senators
Honor the fuzz

BadDriversHandbook@AOL.com

C'mon Detroit : It's So Simple

All we want is: a car that looks like a cross between a
shark and a spaceship, that gets 100 miles to a gallon, that
cruises at 100 mph and that costs under $5,000.

If God had wanted us to go slow-
(S)He wouldn't have given us a gas pedal shaped like a foot.

**Everyone should drive five lengths behind the car in
front of them**—so I can cut in.

REAL BAD DRIVERS:

Don't just match the speed limits—they exceed them.
Don't hafta look both ways at intersections-
they're only going one way.
Can always make a yellow light.
Don't stop for red lights—
even when they're on the top of another car.
Don't signal for turns—they know where the hell they're going.
Know the 55 mph speed limit was a
commie plot to sap our vitality.
Think windshield wipers are for sissies.

BAD DRIVERS MOTTOES

Always be polite to other drivers—
it gives them a false sense of security.
If you drive fast enough the radar can't catch you.
Why do those other morons slow down from
55 to 45 when they see a parked cop car?
Either you crush other drivers or they crush you.
If it was my car do you think I'd be driving like this?
IF they don't want us to park on the sidewalk, why isn't there
a sign that says, "Don't park on the sidewalk"?
If I didn't want the right of way I wouldn't have a big car.
Driving lessons are for wimps.
The closer you drive to the person in front of you the faster
you can encourage them to go.

ALTHOUGH
WE ARE PERFECT,
WE SOMETIMES ENGINEER
MISTAKES TO ALLIEVIATE
BOREDOM.

Slow Drivers
Can be cured
Without a doubt
Honk your horn
Scream and shout!

THE BAD DRIVER'S QUESTIONNAIRE

In order to more fully understand who you are we ask you to take this little quiz about who you think you are. It shouldn't take more than a couple hours.

NAME...Alias ....
Fake name you give at accidents ....
Fake name on your fake ID..
Name your Momma called you ....
Nickname you would like to be called..
Nickname you are actually called..
SuperHero Name..
ADDRESS ....
No kidding—you really live in a vacant lot? ....
Have you lived here less than 3 days? Yes............No...........
Last known address...
Address where you actually pick up your mail ....
Address where you want your 10 million Dollars Publisher's
Sweepstakes check delivered...
Address where, Dog the Bounty Hunter, can find you? ....
CELL PHONE NUMBER..
Last cell phone #...........................One before that ....
Disposable cell phone #.................Untraceable #................................
Do you have a girl friend or boy friend? Yes...........No...........
Are they hot? Are they easy? Phone # ?...
Wife or husband or "friend"? Are they hot? ....
Are they easy? Phone? ....
Do you have a Mother? Address...
Would she pay a ransom over $10,000 for you? ....
Would you pay a ransom over $10,000 for her? ....
Is she easy? Is she hot? Her Phone? ....
YOUR AGE...........No, your real age...........
SEX Yes...........No...........
HOBBIES.................................Other lame pastimes ....
NUMBER OF CRASHES THIS WEEK................YESTERDAY ....
NUMBER OF TICKETS THIS WEEK?................TODAY?..................

*You can make a copy of these 2 pages of this book to give to your relatives or friends to see if they could be helped by the **Bad Driver's Handbook.***

LAST WILL AND TESTAMENT ....

....

Who gets your Mercedes? ....

Who gets your iPad? ....

Who gets your Vibrator? ....

Who gets your Big Wheels? ....

Who gets your Ticket collection? ....

Who gets your GPS? ....

Who gets your Bad Drivers Handbook? ....

Who gets your naughty tapes? ....

DO YOU LIKE GLADIATOR MOVIES? Yes............No...........

DO YOU LIKE BEACH BLANKET MOVIES? Yes...........No...........

DO YOU MISS NELLIE BLY? Yes...........No...........

DO YOU MISS SHEENA, QUEEN OF THE JUNGLE?
Yes...........No...........

DO YOU MISS XENA, WARRIOR PRINCESS? Yes...........No...........

WOULD YOU DATE LARA CROFT? Yes...........No...........

WOULD YOU DATE BRUCE CAMPBELL, THE CHIN?
Yes...........No...........

DO YOU LIKE MOVIES WITH NAKED ANIMALS? Yes.......No.........

DO YOU LIKE NAKED ANIMALS WITH MOVIES? Yes.......No.........

WOULD YOU HAVE A SMOKE WITH A FURRY? Yes.......No...........

HOW OFTEN DO YOU THINK SOMEONE SHOULD
BE WHIPPED?

HOW LONG WOULD YOU SWIM IN JELL-O? ....

EVER BEEN TO A DUNGEON? Yes.......No.......

DID YOU PAY THEM? Yes.......No.......DID THEY PAY YOU?
Yes......No.......

HAVE YOU EVER DONE IT ON A UNICYCLE? Yes.......No.......

DO YOU THINK BIG TRUCKS ARE ROMANTIC? Yes.......No.......

DO YOU BELIEVE IN CAPITAL PUNISHMENT? Yes.......No.......

WHICH CAPITAL DO YOU PREFER?.......

HAVE YOU EVER DATED A TV OR MOVIE STAR? Yes.......No...........

THEIR NAME ....

ARE THEY HOT? Yes.......No......

THEIR PRIVATE PHONE # ....

EVER DATED A POLITICIAN? Yes.......No.......

GOT ANY DIRT ON THEM? Yes.......No.......

WHAT'S IT WORTH? $ .... NEED HELP COLLECTING?
Yes......No.......

WHAT NATIONALITY ARE YOU?...........WHAT SPECIES?................

*Thank you for filling out the BAD DRIVER QUESTIONNAIRE form. We will review your
answers and if we like them we'll get back to you.
Don't hold your breath . . .*

PSYCHOLOGICAL PROFILE FORM

Fill out this simple form to find out how far you differ from the norm. Choose the description that comes the closest to your weird thoughts and mark it down on your arm so you can hand it in later.

1   If your neighbor buys a shiny new car your reaction is:
A   To block his driveway.
B   To spray paint the car windows.
C   Order a truckload of manure dumped on it.
D   Hijack it and leave it in the hood.
E   Stuff it with elephant parts.

2   If someone *threatens* to sue you, you would:
A   Hide their remote.
B   Shoot them in the knees.
C   Shave their body and dip them in hot wax.
D   Remove their kidneys and feed them cola.
E   Kidnap them and sell them to slavers.

3   If someone criticized your driving, you would:
A   Drive a spike thru their TV remote.
B   Criticize their ensemble and makeup.
C   Trick them onto a Reality show.
D   Take them for a ride in your trunk.
E   Lock them in a (hungry) tiger's cage.

4   Your favorite dream is:
A   Being a slave in a bordello.
B   Riding a camel thru a convent.
C   Driving a 3 Decker bus thru wet donuts.
D   Falling into a butterscotch pie.
E   Being a turquoise jelly bean.

5   If anyone *touches* your car you will:
A   Scold them.
B   Hide their fingers.
C   Take away their breathing privileges.
D   Punish them *severely* unto the 7th generation.
E   Make them take this exam.

6   If you were eaten by a polar bear, where would it dump you?
    A   On the Frozen Waste Dumping Ground.
    B   At the entrance to an igloo.
    C   On the local Seals patio.
    D   In downtown Nome.
    E   At the nearest open gas station.
    F   In the BBQ of the local political emporium.

7   If you were reborn as a bus you would:
    A   Head for Vegas.
    B   Have clothing optional.
    C   Have a cop and taxi swatter.
    D   Have air horns on every side.
    E   Have automatic ejection seats.
    F   Not stop for anyone.

8   If someone blasts you with their bad rap music, you:
    A   Give them a gang sign.
    B   Play yours louder.
    C   Break out the booze.
    D   Run them off the road.
    E   Plan a drive-by.
    F   Head for Vegas.

9   If you won a million dollars you would:
    A   Buy a million dollar sports car.
    B   Buy two half million sports cars.
    C   Buy three $333,333.33 sports cars.
    D   Buy four $250,000 sports cars.
    E   Buy five $200,000 sports cars.
    F   Talk to Jay Leno about buying cars.

10 If you were on a soap opera you would be:
    A   Jezebel the Evil twin of Roscoe the Rosicrucian.
    B   Micah the traitor to Candyland and PO'd pedophile.
    C   Donk, the 3rd wife of Grizelda Farkle, king of Burly.
    D   Yahoo, the devil-may-care offspring of the pot Duke.
    E   Patty the Pickle, Queen ruler of far off Noodlestan and
        pledged to wed and govern forever in the cursed Land of
        Silage, where the prince who may not be named, lies hiding
        in a coma. Whew.

11 If you were a ballerina and your tutu was loose, you would:
    A   Staple it back on.
    B   Use duct tape to repair it.
    C   Cinch it up with baling wire.
    D   Repair it with Epoxy and sand paper.
    E   Scream piercingly and demand a better one.

12 If you were trapped in a Saharan sandstorm, would you:
    A   Cut open your Bedouin burka and crawl inside?
    B   Cut open your camel and crawl inside?
    C   Cut open your neighbor and crawl inside?
    D   Dig a hole in the sand, crawl in and pull the hole in after you?
    E   Hop on your Segway and head for the nearest oasis?

13 If you were a politician and someone attached you to a lie detector, would you:
    A   Explode in a cloud of crap?
    B   Commit Kalahari on the machine?
    C   Refuse to answer, comment or breathe?
    D   Explain that you were a Luddite and had to go?
    E   Give a long winded irrational diatribe on nothing?

14 If you were trapped in an elevator, who would you eat first?
    A   A nun.
    B   A lawyer.
    C   A parasitologist.
    D   A TV preacher.
    E   A used car salesman.
    F   A hippopotamus.

Your psychological profile from taking this test has been automatically transmitted to a secret hidden underground Repository 3 miles east of Reston Wa. Where it will be calibrated, postulated, segregated, intubated and folded by hypmotized Gov. minion droids who will bedevaluate and destroy it thru the Furguson Process of belittleling. Lucky for you.(You pervert you)

You can tell your muffler's going when you can't sneak up on pedestrians anymore.

I Drive Like Hell because:

- I'm ME.
- I have a gun.
- The cops are after me.
- I'm late for a bar opening.
- My car is almost nearly paid for.
- I am nearly a name in moviedom.
- I know a guy who knows a guy who met Sinatra.
- I don't know what's wrong with my GPS.
- I think my brakes are going.
- My nails are almost dry.
- My nails are pretty.
- I need air.
- There's a gawdamn bee in the car and it's trying to psych me out.

Who has the Right of Way at an Accident?

A The News crews
B The Papa-rot-zzi
C The Rubber neckers
D A blabby neighbor
E NCIS
F The coroner

The squatting dinosaurs on our highways should be extincted.

The New
LASER METER 2050

YOU SHOULDN'T GIVE ME A TICKET OFFICER, BECAUSE:

- I already have dozens of tickets I can't pay.
- I don't have room in the trunk for any more cops bodies.
- My boss doesn't know that I borrowed his car.
- The last cop left me off with a warning and I don't have any more money for 'tips'.
- It's an emergency, I have a sick squirrel in the glove compartment.
- If I'm late, I'll miss the opening strippers best number.
- I tried to stop for the light but my brakes wouldn't work.
- We're going to the drive-in and my wife and kids are in the trunk.
- I thought that sign was a "GO" sign.
- My glasses were fogged up and I couldn't tell what color the light was.
- The Godfather will be P. O.'ed if I'm late with his stuff.
- My doctor says I only have a year left so I have to drive fast wherever I go.
- I wasn't waving my middle finger at you, I was winding it up to pick my nose, honest.

BAD DRIVERS HINTS

A good driver signals for turns, a really good driver doesn't have to signal.

If you see someone in trouble—wave.

If your brakes fail—use pedestrians to slow you down.

55 mph is a good safe speed in a 25 mph zone.

Hitch-hiking is dangerous and it's up to the responsible driver to prove it to the hitch-hiker.

If someone blocks you in a parking space add a little sugar to their gas tank to make their driving sweeter.

**It's okay to have crazy friends,
Just do not let them into your car,
And N E V E R let them drive!**

THE TOP 10 EXCUSES FOR BEING LATE

10 We were in an ambulance mishap and we were all night trying to catch the guy on the gurney.

9 We were making out in the front seat and just at the best part a cop stopped us.

8 My radio is broke so I had to drive beside somebody that had my station on.

7 My windshield wipers don't work so I had to backup the whole way.

6 I fell asleep at the wheel and when I woke up I was inanother state.

5 Some knucklehead in front of me slowed down to pass an accident.

4 I had to slow down to check out a 10 car pileup for bodies.

3 Somebody put a fence across my favorite shortcut.

2 I not only got a flippin ticket, I got a flippin lecture.

1 I couldn't just leave him laying in the street.

THE TOP TEN REASONS WHY I DIDN'T PASS MY DRIVER'S TEST:

10 They asked all kinds of stupid questions about hospitals and speed limits.

9 She misinterpreted my hand signals when I put my arm around her.

8 It took me eight tries and two bumpers to parallel park.

7 The officer was a sorehead because I backed into his patrol car.

6 I guess the bigoted SOB didn't like ethnic jokes.

5 You tell a woman how much you really admire her big boobs and this is the thanks you get.

4 They didn't say they subtracted points for running over the instructor's feet.

3 How was I to know the raised middle finger was not a valid hand signal?

2 You offer an officer a friendly swig of booze and see what it gets you.

1 Its fixed.

I HAVE THE RIGHT OF WAY BECAUSE:

I'm late.   I'm early.

My brakes aren't working right.

I'm going fast enough.   There's no one in the back seat.

There's someone in the back seat. I have my turn signal on.

I'm wearing a baseball cap.   I'm wearing a leisure suit.

I just got a new outfit.   I'm naked.

I'm worried about something else.

I have a stupid little yellow sign on my windshield.

I have an odd numbered license plate.

Somebody's waiting for me.

Nobody's waiting for me.

I HAVE THE RIGHT OF WAY BECAUSE: #2

I have my turn signal off.

I'm old and grumpy.

I'm young and quick.

My car's all paid for.

This is a borrowed car.

Me belong to Menza.

I belong to Roadrunners.™

I am a visitor to this state.

I am a visitor to this country.

I am a strange visitor from another planet.

I have a St Christopher medal.

I have a Buddha statue.

I have a Roadrunner statue.

I have a statue of Cthulhu.

I remember the Alamo.

I remember Pearl Harbor.

I remember to take out the garbage.

I watch Big Bang religiously.

I Big Bang religiously.

I'm out of pretzels.

I'm out of KY.

Oh no, even more . . .

I HAVE THE RIGHT OF WAY BECAUSE: #3

My insurance is all paid up.
My insurance has lapsed.
My dad's the mayor.
I have a death wish.
I lost my death wish and don't know where to find it.
I found my death wish under the couch.
I have fresh eggs in the back seat.
I have old dynamite in the trunk.
My car cost more than yours.
My car is cheaper than yours.
My popcorn on the radiator is almost ready to pop.
My girlfriend in the back seat is almost ready to pop.
The cop in the backseat is, you guessed it, ready to pop.
My left rear tire is ready to pop.
I had all the pop I could take and now I gotta P.
I hadda P and now I'm too pooped to pop.

And just when you thought you were safe---

I HAVE THE RIGHT OF WAY BECAUSE: #4

My dog is helping me drive.
I am legally blind.
I can't afford to be late again.
I have frozen food in the trunk.
I have frozen bodies in the trunk.
The cops are chasing me.
I'm almost out of gas.
I have my turn signal on.
I am an SOB.
I am a big SOB.
I am a really big SOB.
I'm the biggest SOB on the road.

Pedestrians are an Endangered Species when I'm behind the wheel.

IT'S OKAY TO GO FASTER THAN THE SPEED LIMIT IF:

Your father-in-law is the mayor.

You are the mayor.

You have something incriminating on the Police Chief.

You haven't had very many wrecks before.

You have a Support-your-Local-Police bumper sticker.

You think you left the water running at home.

You're driving a very big truck.

You think your engine might be on fire.

Your engine IS on fire.

You're on fire.

You're pregnant.

You're going to see someone that wants to be pregnant.

You've already seen this scenery.

Your horoscope said this is a good-day for speeding.

You have a lucky St. Christopher medallion on your dash.

THE FASTER YOU GO-

The more gas you save.

The faster you can stop.

The faster you can see danger.

The faster your responses have to be.

The more efficiently your motor works.

The quicker you get to your final destination.

THERE ARE TWO KINDS OF REALLY BAD DRIVERS-

Ones that always believe that they have
the right of way-
and ones that believe that everyone else
has the right of way.

"Give me one *good* reason why I should give you **my** car so you can go out joy riding with your friends."

"Well, Dad, I don't know what you do on your business trips but I found these panties under the front seat and they're not Moms."

"Here's the keys and fifty bucks, please be careful."

"I will, you too, Dad."

"One more for the road, Barkeep."

"Okay, but gimme the keys to your car first. I gotta protect the other people out there driving tonight. My wife and family might be out there. My girlfriend might be out there. They might meet."

In bumper to bumper traffic the left lane will be the faster moving lane—unless you're in it.

Most drivers *know* that, all other things being equal, they have the right of way.

BAD DRIVERS HANDBOOK BUMPER STICKERS

I brake for . . . nothing.

Warning—Psychopathic Driver

RUNAWAY TRUCKS—USE OTHER LANE

If driving is an art—I'm a friggin Picasso.

You should drive a safe distance behind the car
in front of you—at least three feet.

If you're gonna drive under the speed limit—
you gotta expect people to shoot at you.

When in doubt—pass

If God had wanted us to drive slowly and carefully—
SHe wouldn't have given us horns.

Pedestrians are an endangered species—when I'm on the road

Honk if you're an azzhole.

I flunked my flying exam but I still have my driver's license

HONK IF YOU LOVE QUICK STOPS

Passing me would be a grave error.

This car stops for Planes, Trains and Broads.

I CAN DRIVE FASTER—
CAN YOU STOP FASTER?

Warning: this car swerves to kill shum ditz
and ucking fidiots.

Abandon hope all ye who try to pass me

Going to see a man about a horse

Bumper riders are frustrated sodomists

SUPPORT YOUR LOCAL ASYLUM

**RED means to slow down.
YELLOW is to warn other drivers
you're coming thru.
GREEN means to GUN IT!!!**

SEGWAYS

1 Don't really exist.
2 Are built by gremlins.
3 In a hollow tree.
4 Require 2 triple A batteries.
5 Are afraid of escalators.

Scooters

1 Can run on hair oil.
2 Can be carried in a back seat.
3 Can sneak under an 18 wheeler.
4 Are almost as good as a bike.
5 Can pull an (empty) hay wagon.
6 Carry a whole family in Tokyo.

Motorcycles

1 Need more wheels.
2 Need some kind of umbrella.
3 Make good hood ornaments.
4 Are hard to chase thru trees.
5 Are good for catching bugs.
6 Can run on piss and vinegar.
7 Are fun to ride thru malls.

Mini Coopers

1 Will fit in the trunk.
2 Can be stacked like Legos.
3 Have an extra windup key.
4 Come in Cracker Jack boxes.
5 Can be parked behind the couch

Hummers

1 Require a German accent to access the drive controls.

2 Have a Survivor kit with an M14 and grenades.

3 Have the same fuel consumption as a 707.

4 Have tires made in das Gespitzuntsparkwerks, Austria.

5 Do not require a passport to drive from state to state.

6 Are designed to fit thru most metric tunnels.

7 Have a bullet proof glove compartment and safe.

8 Carry extra ashtrays and a spare engine.

9 Can be equipped with chintz curtains and a gold potty.

10 Are bigger on the inside than the outside.

18 Wheelers

0 Do not float.

1 Have 37 gears and a useless braking system.

2 Are great for intimate two person parties.

3 Have to scrape off birds and bunnies weekly.

4 Can be used to test the weight strength of bridges.

5 May pickup hitch-hikers: on the bumper.

6 Cost more than a medium sized house.

7 Are good for carrying contraband.

8 Have special scoops for VW Bugs and Mini Coopers.

9 Can cross the USA in just two weeks.

10 Often host traveling wild parties.

11 Are driven by studs and dykes with real cajones.

Driving with NO headlights

1 Allows you to drink in the beauty of the night.

2 Lets you sneak up on bikers and runners.

3 Is more fun when you're drunk.

4 Scares the spit out of the kids.

5 Is easier in the daytime.

Hitch-Hikers

1   Should know better.
2   Have to be quick on their feet to survive.
3   Better have some cash to pay for their ride.
4   Need to know their place: on the bumper.
5   If they aren't bisexual—they will be.
6   Are good with a fine Chianti.

Stop Signs

1   Are indicators to slow down a bit and be vigilant.
2   Have nine sides: including the back.
3   Are great for target practice.
4   Are a waste of time.
5   Are fun to collect.
6   All of the above.

Speed Limits

1   Mean nothing in a constantly changing universe.
2   Are a stinky way of collecting unjust revenue.
3   Are usually underrated by a ratio of 3 to 1.
    i.e.: A 20 mph posting is good for 60 mph.
4   Can be doubled for souped up cars.
5   Are relatively relative.
6   Suck.

City Traffic

1   Sells more aspirin.
2   Gives a lot more targets.
3   Helps in planning get-aways.
4   Is more fun than an amusement park.
5   Will someday become a permanent gridlock.
6   Would be a lot better if the lights were all green.
7   Would be perfect if there weren't any buses or trucks.

Back in the 20th century I conceived of a <u>Guide for Bad Drivers</u> book. On a vacation I found I could keep from zoning out while driving long hours by thinking things—Being Absurd, here are 30 things that I thought about:

Bad Driver's Exam

1   If a bicyclist in a fancy uniform is riding on your road—Do you:
A. Bump him.
B. Run him off the road.
C. Run him down.
D. Run him down and beat him up.
E. All of the above and pee on his bike.

2   If you see someone broken down by the roadside—Do you:
A. Give them the finger.
B. Throw garbage at them.
C. Sideswipe them.
D. Offer to help and push them into a ditch.
E. Give them a lift to a garage and go back and strip their car.

3   You are stopped by a State Trooper with spinach in his teeth-Do you:
A. Giggle every time he talks.
B. Lecture him on personal appearance.
C. Ask to take a picture of his smile.
D. Report him to his superior.
E. Slip him a jalapeño on a toothpick.

4   If an oncoming car doesn't dim its lights—Do you:
A   Run him off the road.
B. Throw rocks at his windshield.
C. Shoot out his headlights
D   Follow him home, hide his keys and paint his windshield.

5   If you miss the turn-off sign: How many miles will you go before there is a sign that tells you you're on the wrong road?
A. A hundred friggin miles.
B. A hundred and one friggin miles.
C. There is no sign. You'll just keep going till you drive into the ocean.

6 A County Sheriff can stop and fine you if:
A. His coffee is cold.
B. You have out-of-state plates.
C. Your car is the wrong color.
D. Your skin is the wrong color.
E. You have really hot wheels.
F. He didn't get any last night.

7 On a six lane highway, if a truck is going 50 mph and a bus is passing it at 51 mph and a trailer is passing it at 51.5 mph, how many miles will you go before:
A. You utter your first blasphemous curse.
B. The veins on your forehead become visible.
C. You remember there is a magnum in the glove compartment.
D. You pass on the berm.

8 If you ask for directions in New York City-The most likely answer will be:
A. Sorry, I'm just visiting, I'm lost too.
B. Go down two blocks and turn left. You can't miss it.
C. No hablo Inglis.
D. You #@%& tourists, why don't you #@%& your*&%y @$$!
E. All of the above.

9 Its okay to pass on a blind curve if:
A. You have good insurance.
B. You're talking on the phone.
C. You have more than one six-pack onboard.
D. Your lover just dumped you.
E.The bar might close if you're late.

10 If that drink you threw out the window hit a motorcyclist in the face—Your best move is to give him the finger and:
A. Throw your wallet in his face, too.
B. Hit an abutment.
C. Climb out on the hood and moon him to earn his respect.
D. Shoot yourself before he does.

11 Who has the right of way?
A. The vehicle that's paid off.   B,The fastest vehicle.
C. The biggest vehicle.   D.The heaviest vehicle.
E. The driver with the biggest nads.

12 If someone cuts you off—Do you:
A. Flip them the bone.
B. Nudge them.
C. Cut them off and back into them.
D. Follow them home, burn their car, shoot their dog and steal their identity.

13 If the speed limit is seventy mph and you've been driving 68 mph for two hundred miles and you speed up to 71 mph to pass a truck, when will you pass the State Trooper?
Haven't you been paying attention?
Do this one over until you get it.

WHAT? even MORE Bad Driver's Exam?

14 The big guy you ran off the road is in IHOP when you go in— Do you:
A. Spill coffee on his bandaged eye.
B. Make a pass at his wife and daughter.
C. Slap him on his back brace, give him a hug and lift his wallet.
D. Go back and let the air out of his tires and put glue in his keyholes.

15 The Maximum speed limit is:
A. What's posted plus 20.
B. What's posted plus 60.
C. What's posted plus 100.
D. Whatever's possible.
E. The World's Land Speed Record plus 20.

16 At an intersection:
A. All other cars should stop and let me thru.
B. All other cars better stop and let me thru.
C. All other cars must stop and let me thru.
D. I have the right of way because I'm driving *my* car.

17 Driving in the city requires:
A. Courage.   B. Talent.   C. Coordination.   D. Nads.

18 If you drink a Super big Gulp every 20 minutes, what are your chances of making it to a rest area before you wet the seat?
A. 0.   B. 1%.   C. 1.1%.   D. Ooops.

19 If car A (The Fast) leaves Vegas going 120 mph and car B (The Furious) leaves Chicago going 160 mph—Where will they meet?
A. Tijuana, Mexico.
B. Hell, Montana.
C. Froggy's Bar, Daytona Beach, FL.
D. San Quentin.
E. Betty Ford Clinic.

20 The trailer hitch on the car in front of you is breaking loose—Do you:
A. Pull up beside them and challenge them to a drag race.
B. Call the TV station and ask if they pay for accident reports.
C. Get the camera ready.
D. Pull in front of them and drive crazily so they don't notice when the trailer breaks off, so you can go back and loot it.

21 An eight-sided red stop sign says:
A. Slow down a bit.
B. Time for another beer.
C. This is as good a place as any to finish the bj.
D. Watch for pedestrians carrying things that might scratch your car when you hit them.

22 How many onion burritos does it take to clear out a medium sized car?   A - 1   B - .5

23 You have a blowout and start to lose control of your car-Do you:
A. Give yourself the finger.
B. Scream and wet your pants.
C. Aim for the most expensive nearby vehicle.
D. Jump into the backseat where it's safer.

24 A four way stop sign means:
A. You have the right of way.
B. Other cars have to stop for you.
C Go, go, go.
D. You have the right of way.
E. You have four choices.
F. You should drive off in all four directions.

25 Drinking while driving:
A. Requires a good cup holder to prevent spillage.
B. Is better than peeing while driving.
C. Turns the morning commute from frustrating to fun.
D. Is okay if you go fast enough to be scared and alert.

26 Never pick up hitch-hikers:
A Unless they're female.
B. Unless they're topless.
C. Unless they're DD.
D. Unless they're naked.
E. Unless you're too drunk to drive.

27 Your horn:
A. Gives you the right of way.
B. Is there to scare pedestrians.
C. Is better than the finger.
D. Can signal other drivers to get out of your way.
E. Can be used to speed up other cars or clear up traffic jams.

28 You've just caused a five car pileup—Do you:
A. Try to sell insurance to the survivors.
B. Say you have a hot date and drive off.
C. Give a fake ID to the cop, and say, "No spik Engrish."
D. Pretend to be unconscious so you can steal the gear from the ambulance.

29 You're rocketing along at 95 mph and hear a siren—Do you:
A. Look around to see who is in trouble.
B. Pull over, put on your seat belt and try to hide the bottles.
C. Scan your excuse list on the sun visor.
D. Pull out a fifty, fold it and palm it to slip it to the cop.
E. Tuck your magnum under your right leg.

30 The best way to get a slow driver out of the fast lane is:
A. The Horn.
B The Finger.
C A Nudge.
D All of the above at once. **End of the Exam: Go home.**

I want to believe you- can't you tell me
more convincing lies?

You can't Give Me a ticket, Officer because:

- My parents will absolutely KILL me.
- The cat just peed on my leg.
- I'm almost out of gas.
- I did not see the sign.
- They warned me.
- Nobody told me.
- My dad's a Republican.
- My mom's a Democrat.
- My uncles an excon.
- My great aunt met a guy who talked to George Clooney's hairdresser.

Four Cars arrive at a 4 way crossroad—Who goes first?

A   The Shiniest.
B   The Biggest.
C   The Latest model.
D   The one that's paid off.
E   The most drunk one.
F   None of the above.
G   And none of the below.
H   I really don't know and
I   don't care.

You can't arrest me because:

- There's a sale on and I'm late.
- My boy friend needs a drink.
- I have my good shoes on.
- I definitely need a drink.
- Do you want a drink?
- The dog has hiccups.
- You'll be sorry, I betcha.
- You can't look in the trunk!
- It would violate my civil rights.
- I hafta take Gramma to the hospital. Gramma! Where the heck is she?

Wha???

"Where's Bruce?"
He went away.
"Did he say where he was going?"
No, all he said was. 'Woops.'
"Explain."
We were having a contest to see who could get closest to the passing big trucks on the highway and Bruce won. He's probably in Chicago by now.

"I don't usually stop for hitch-hikers but when I saw you waving your bra I knew you needed help."

"But officer, why do I have to be blindfolded and on my knees to take a breathalyzer test?"

Your tortellini has too many torts.

Evel Knievel Jr jumps a box of Cheetos

Bad Driver's
Laptop Computer
Allows Calculations up to 21
Coed Model to 22

Top 10 Reasons Why I can Drive BAD:

10 The faster I go the quicker I get there.

9 I have double credit at the hospital.

8 I have PMS, testosterone and GPS.

7 The Jr Woodchucks have no fear.

6 My insurance is comprehensive.

5 Satan taught me how to drive.

4 My drugs are still hitting.

3 I'm ready for a new car.

2 I'm tired of living.

1 Nobody cares.

Hey fuzznutz;

You have to drive faster than I do to catch me and give me a speeding ticket.

Get the irony?

Everything is harder than it is.

W.T.F.: Things that might indicate you're a bad Driver:

⅄ The Hollywood Stunt Driver's Association burnt your application.

⅄ Your Driver's license is invalid in 51 states, 3 territories, 10 provinces and 212 countries.

⅄ Chuck Norris is afraid to ride with you.

⅄ The area around your home town is a no fly zone.

⅄ Your Lawyer firm of Weal, Cheatem and Howe have given up the legal profession and opened an emu ranch.

⅄ You have put three Insurance companies out of business.

⅄ Even your car is afraid of you and sometimes hides in other peoples garages.

⅄ Dracula said he'd rather drink wine than your blood.

⅄ The World Wrasslin' Confederation said all the stuff people say about you is probably true.

⅄ China is extending the Great Wall specifically to keep you out.

⅄ The Navy Seals refused to give protective cover for you.

⅄ Australia changed its immigration laws to bar undesirables, mentioning you in particular.

⅄ They closed three of your favorite highways just because you use them.

⅄ International Traffic laws have a whole chapter on WHY you are not allowed passage.

⅄ When asked to help you, the A-Team said, "No way."

⅄ The Barnum & Bailey circus cancelled your Dare—Devil Act when they couldn't find ANY insurance anywhere to cover it.

⅄ Evel Knievel retired because of you.

⅄ The Moon Shot was delayed a week because they heard you *might* be driving thru Florida.

⅄ In Transylvania they scare the kids with stories about you.

W.T.F.2: More Things that
indicate you're a Bad Driver:

⅄ The neighbors grab their kids and pets and run inside when your garage door opens.

⅄ A new electronic remote vehicle stopping device is named after you.

⅄ All traffic has been rerouted away from your section of town.

⅄ You are on a first name basis with everyone in Traffic Court.

⅄ Your GPS directions are rebroadcast on all police bands.

⅄ Ex cons have been warned about associating with you.

⅄ Hitchhikers hide from you.

⅄ The only foreign passport you can get is for Antarctica.

⅄ The three Driving Schools you went to have gone broke.

⅄ Your psychiatrist has given up his practice and gone into beekeeping.

⅄ The FBI has taken you off their *Person of Interest* list and put you on their *Least Wanted* list.

⅄ Nobody on Facebook 'likes' you: in fact they added a new option that only applies to you: "Hate".

⅄ The Republicans AGREED with the Democrats that your driver's license should be revoked.

⅄ The devil has a shrine to *you*.

Quotes

"I like tunnels, they make good places for ambushes."

Psychopath One

"I love to drive in the country, there are more road targets; bunnies, cats, groundhogs, raccoons, deer, cows, farmers, wagons, barns, silos, giant water tanks."

Psychopath Two

Bad Driver Pledges:
I hereby resolve:

➤ To always go faster than anyone else.

➤ To never give way to other drivers.

➤ To never let other drivers cut in.

➤ To cut corners, curves and sidewalks.

➤ To drive in my middle of the road.

➤ To never give warning signals.

➤ To scare the crap out of joggers.

➤ To outrun the radar.

➤ To bully smaller cars and cycles.

➤ To drive like hell til get there.

➤ To make my own shortcuts.

➤ To never dim my lights.

➤ To drive my car into the ground.

➤ To scare the spit out of my passengers.

➤ To stay lost before I'll ask for directions.

➤ To treat my car like a stupid machine.

➤ To park wherever I want.

➤ To drive forever in circles.

I am King of the Road because:

I'm hot.
My car is hot.
I have insurance.
I have a real GPS.
I can pee standing up.
My car is about paid up.
I have a zombie whacker.
My road taxes are paid up.
I possess 32 credit cards.
My car has a land anchor.
I have built-in seat levelers
I have a solid oak gun rack.
I have a redneck BBQ apron.
I have my bull dog beside me.
I know every shortcut in town.
I just won a year of free tattoos.
I shook hands with Bobby Vinton.
I have a gift card from a junk yard.
I can change a flat in two minutes.
They just named the town dump after me.
I can fix a broken sprocket with my penknife.
I have a super-game streaming, superior iPod,
My car seats six with room in the trunk for eight
bodies. I have 2 car salesmen and a worried hitch-
hiker in the trunk now. I've got a double whammy
barreled carburetor and a 30G flumox . . . Including
a triple Z booster, touch smart controls, a midi pyre
multifunctional integrated KY speakers and self-
emptying ashtrays.

I am Queen of the Road because

I'm cool.♥
Forget PMS.♥
My car is cool.♥
I've got coverage♥
I got an Oprah hug.♥
I do not need a GPS♥
I have 32 credit cards♥
My bra is bullet proof.♥
I have a rug rat muffler♥
With a built-in massager♥
I know where the bodies are.♥
I am regal in my driving togs.♥
I have connections high and low.♥
I have a special Rachel Raye spoon.♥
I know every ice cream shop in town.♥
I can pee without removing my clothes.♥
I have a massaging recliner in my hot tub.♥
I can start a car with the key in my mouth. ♥
I know who has skeletons in their closets.♥
I have a thousand ways to get what I want. ♥
My brother-in-law runs an Auto repair shop.♥
I have a hundred ways to get out of a ticket.♥
I have a close relationship with 4 law offices.♥
I know every Nail Salon, Thrift Store and Legal
Aid. I can fix a broken sprocket with a hairpin ♥ and
fingernail file. ♥ I have a hitch-hiker and two sales
guys locked in my trunk now.♥ I have the Buddha,
St. Christopher, Mickey Mouse and MR. SpongeBob
Squarepants on my dash.♥

POTPOURRI

Potpourri popʊ'ri:/ *is a mixture of dried* plant *material, used to provide a natural scent, It is usually tied in a small* sachet.

The word "potpourri" comes into English from the French *word "potpourri." Literally, the word "pot" in French has the same meaning as it does in Spanish and English, while the word "pourri" means* **rotten.** *In English, "potpourri" is often used to refer to* any collection *of miscellaneous or diverse items.*

Ed:sorry, I got carried away on this definition from Wikipedia.

So Literally potpourri means a stinky collection of rotten items. Boy, that's us. Here they are:

When racing a train to a crossing—winning or losing is not important as long as its NOT A TIE.

Just because you're at the head of a line of traffic doesn't mean you're the Leader of the Pack.

You can make up for time lost in traffic by honking your horn.

LEAVING YOUR BRIGHTS ON ALL THE TIME REMINDS OTHER DRIVERS TO DIM THEIRS.

A SCARED DRIVER IS A CAUTIOUS DRIVER AND EASIER TO OUTMANEUVER.

I always obey the speed limits- but my 55 mph is a lot faster than your 55 mph.

Why I have a Turret on the Roof of my Car:

- It wouldn't fit on my bike.
- They had a sale on, buy one-get one free.
- Other cars have their gun racks, this is mine.
- It's a neat little idea I picked up in the service.
- State law says it can only be mounted on a roof.
- The Boy Scout's motto fits: BE PREPARED.
- It bothers me when other drivers don't dim their lights.
- Giving the finger and swearing are just not enough to teach some poor drivers their place.
- You never can tell when we'll have to fight back against space aliens.
- Sometimes you just have to have protection against the unknown.
- You might be out driving and be attacked by an angry bull.
- I'm ready to protect my country, no matter what it takes.
- What do you use to take out a flock of alligators?
- Wanna see its night vision tracking system?
- Its much more persuasive than a shotgun.
- It came with a complete GI Joe army set.
- It's a family legacy from Uncle Adolph.
- I can control it remotely with my iPad.
- It even has a built-in sniper scope.
- The cops have radar—I have this.
- I was the highest bidder on eBay.
- It shoots cast iron bowling balls.
- It took a ton of coupons.
- It's a babe magnet.

Cougars in Jaguars chasing a Greyhound

NoNo's

I Became a [Used] CAR Salesman because:

I love the smell of new cars.
I needed the $$$ but I hate the work.
My wife wasn't making enough for my lifestyle.
I love cars and I need a free repair shop.
I need a clean cover for my drug business.
I am a people person, the more people I meet the more I
    can screw.
My Patrone said he needed me in a quiet undercover
    occupation.
Money isn't everything-but it's a start.
I like having the pick of the top models to drive.
My folks said they were going to kick me out if I didn't get
    a job.
I already tried out being an astronaut and a brain
    surgeon.
I was too big to be a jockey and too short to be a
    basketball player.
The Harlem Globetrotters said I was too white.
My work as a shepherd ended when wolves ate my
    sheep.
The waiting line for Disney CEO was too long.(8 mi.)
I'm working my way up to bagboy at Kmart.
The top position at Tromp Enterprises was already taken
    by a yak merkin.
This is just part-time—I'm also a graffiti artist.
My tag is Sloppy Topper.
My car broke down and I'm trying to get rid of it.
Pickins are really cutthroat in the catfish business.
I tried selling used Fighter Jets door to door and went
    broke.

I Lost my Job as a [used] CAR Salesman Because:

I hate to work.

I didn't make enough in tips.

My life style disagreed with my job.

I didn't sell anything, I just drove the cars around.

They fired me for screwing around on the Job and sleeping in the Cougar. I miss her.

My Kool Aid stand conflicted with my selling cars.

It's the fault of recent economic downturns.

I got busted.

I screwed the *wrong* people.

I guess I stole too many paper clips.

It's not a good idea to hump the bosses wife even when he's humping yours.

Too many 'test drive' wrecks.

I guess it's against company policy to 'rent out' cars that aren't even being used.

I guess I kinda 'lost' a couple cars.

Business expense accounts are not supposed to cover personal vacations,—this aint congress.

I guess I shouldn't have tried to short change my boss on his share of the drug profits.

I couldn't sell any cars when I was locked up in jail.

They apparently didn't like me *screwing* the customers literally. (without a sale)

I guess you're not supposed to lend out new cars to your buddies for drag races.

They threw me out for sticking my talleywacker in the Car Polisher.

They fired the Car Polisher, too.

MORE BUMPER STICKERS

Honk if you like quick stops

Hang up and Drive

Beauty is in the eye
of the beer holder

Faster, faster, thrill, thrill

Please do not distract the driver
while he is acquiring a target

WHEN PRAYER FAILS USE YOUR HORN

Free the Indianapolis 500

Even Mario Andretti
has his bad days

The shortest distance between
two points is ME

WARNING: PSYCHOPATHIC DRIVER

God's greatest gift was the gas pedal: next
was the horn

Spot the Misteaks

A good drivir can see wen someting bad mite hapen: a bad drivur vvill
drivf rite off the bridge . . .

2+2= 5

E=MC3

Is a bear catholick?

driving is a grate life.

55 mph is faster than 55 kmh

Potatoes come from Iraland.

Driving to fast is dangerouss.

Why aren't their any 'GO' signs?

Does the pope poop in the woods?

"chicken" is a national sport in the USA.

Republicans love democrats & vice versa.

This line is a filller and has know mestakes.

The world speed record is held by delorean.

The 1964 land speed record is held by evel knievel.

Pleeze cansel my perscription to yore dum magazine.

A vehicle going 55 mph can stop in 2 car lengths.

this line is not in the bad drivers handbook.

Talleyrand discovered the gulf of mexico.

Henery Ford invented the assambly line.

Baby ruth was a great line driver.

The last statement was true.

the preceding line is false.

Bad drivers are the best.

I just made that up.

All lies are true.

Except this one

and

Wear are the ansers?

Turn the book upside down for the answers.

Just kidding, give yourself whatever score you want—
there are no right answers in this world.

I Can't Go to jail right now officer because:

I have Nothing to wear.
I just have too much to do.
I'll lose my parking space.
All my coupons will expire.
Friday night is Bowling night.
Who would water my plants?
Who would feed my tarantulas?
My neighbors expecting a baby.
We have reservations in Vegas!
My parole officer would miss me.
My banana bunch would go bad.
I can't make it without my soaps.
Mom said I can't go out anymore.
My guppies need continuous love.
I don't look good in day glow orange.
The Klan meeting is every Thursday.
The girl tied up in the cellar will starve.
My subscription to TV Guide might end.
I have a dreamy date setup for Saturday.
I have a number of scores to settle before I
   can leave.
They might put me in a cell with the cop
that turned me in.
I have a load of . . . uh . . . supplies that will
be arriving shortly.

DRIVERNITIONS

Beer Rack: On the ceiling with a feeding tube.

Bumper Sticker: A sign of mental disturbance.

Construction Zone: Replacing my Destruction Zone

Denver Boot: Gives a very bumpy ride.

Dork: An uninsured driver.

Emergency Brake: You can tell if it's engaged by the smell.

Flat Cat Frisbee: Recycling road kill.

GPS: A lantern in the Land of the Lost.

Guard Rails: To help guide you when you're sleepy.

Heavy Psychedelics: For dealing with heavy traffic.

Hotrod: The car or the driver?

Humvee: They wouldn't sell me a tank.

Knee Grips: For driving 'no hands'.

Las Vegas: Sodom to Hollywood's Gomorrah.

Macho Law: Prohibits me from asking directions.

Outside Speakers: Share your bad taste with the world.

PMS & Migraine: Justifiable homicide.

Pigeons: City skeet.

Pit Stop: When you just have to pit.

Pussy Whipped: The kitty fell in the cream container.

Rest Stops: Red lights.

Relief Tube: Everybody comes with a built in one.

Road Signs: Redneck target practice.

Road Kill: Free snacks for the taking.

Safe Driving Distance: For some drivers-4' behind a garage door.

Safe Driving Speed: –55mph . . . in a 25 mph zone.

Seat Belts: You shouldn't drive crazy without them.

Speed Trap: Where you keep your speed.

Speed Zone: Where you take your uppers.

Traffic Circle: An intersection with no intersection.

Target Acquisition: Another app for your on-board computer.

Underpass: Bikers umbrella.

What If?

What If you took a driver's test and flunked?
A I'd follow the examiner home and report him to his mother.
B I'd examine what I did carefully and discuss it at length with the examiner then punch him in the nose.
C I'd scream and yell and slam doors and curse the examiner, then I'd trash his car.
D I'd thank the examiner politely and go sit in my car. When he came out again I'd run him down.
E I'd tell the examiner what a @#$%^ dolt he was and set fire to his eyebrows.

What if? You got a Ticket for Spitting?
A I would be really displeased.
B I would give up spitting.
C I'd install an expectoration tube on my steering wheel.
D I'd spit on the ticket. Then I'd spit on the cop car, then I'd spit on the cop, then I'd spit on the inside of the cop car, then I'd spit on my jail cell.

What if?
A mad hornet flew into my car when I was going 90 mph?
A I'd try to smash him with my beer can without spilling any.
B I'd throw open my door, jump out and tuck and roll.
C I'd steer with my knees and use my steering wheel lock bar to smash it to smithereens.
D I'd write a nasty letter to the ASPCB*.
   *American Society for the Prevention of Cruelty to Bugs
E I'd close all the windows, light up a stogie and smoke the flying bastid to death.

What if?
I run out of space on this page and try to fake it?
A Uh, you got me on this one.

What If?   2   *(Choose the one that's you)*

What if you ran off the road, into someone's house, thru the house and the car ended up in the Swimming Pool?

A I would pull out a bar of soap and give myself and the car a good scrubbing.

B I would back the car up to the kitchen and ask for directions to the front door.

C I would say, "Sorry." and back out thru the garage wall into the neighbor's rose garden.

D I would strip down to my gutchies and swim a couple laps.

E I would take out my fake bible and offer to baptize everyone in the pool.

What if you accidentally drove off the tenth floor of a parking garage?

A I would look for another parking space on my way down.

B I would turn in my ticket and ask for my money back.

C I would turn in my St Christopher statue and ask for a luckier saint.

D I would be glad I had a good chance to test my air bags.

E I would complain to my dealer that the brakes were useless.

What if you stole a tank on a dare and drove it into a Police Station?

A I'd drive from room to room asking where I could register my weapon.

B I'd drive thru the building to the shooting range and shoot off a couple rounds to blow down the retaining wall.

C I'd ask which way to the mayors' office and did he have enough time to discuss the city's parking problems.

D I'd drive down the hallway into the Restrooms and say, "I'll just be a minute."

E I'd drive thru the Restroom and out and yell, "I'll be back." The restroom would be destroyed and the cops wouldn't know where the hell to go.

Female B.D. Profile *

As horny as they come

GPS earings
the better to ear you with

Nailed it

Thumb thing special

Digital output signal: the universal sign for BS

A real eyeful

Nose what's happening

Loud speaking system

Cold shoulder for the Law

Pussy Horn

Able to bare arms and bear arms

Neon nockers

The Meower Howler
*Born without a horn:
now she has all she wants.*

Lotsa junk in the trunk

Always hip

Convertible camel toe

A sole that needs heeled

Portable Purse Vault
with keys,
Cosmetic kit,
Med kit,
Drugs kit,
First aid kit,
Sex aid kit,
Massage kit,
Unmetionables,
Manacles,
Feathers.

Foot loose and fancy free

PMS detector and sympathizer,
longs for the day when it can
be eradicated

*Her car is her magic carpet
taking her anywhere she wants*

*and/or **Gay/Trans**

Male B.D. Profile *

Bluetooth iPhone with camera, video, vcr, tv, Google GPS

Ear comes the devil

Hair today gone tomorrow

Born with horns: ie-horney

Has a blind eye for speed limits

Ear we go

No arm done

Born to the Horn

Flippin' the bird

Armed and ready

A tale of woe

The nads to get it done

Bad to the bone

Heavy gas foot

His distal phalanges are rank

UTILITY BELT
Tool Kit
Spray paint
Radar detector
Radar deactivator
Itching Powder
Sneezing powder
Stink bombs
Dohickey
Widget
Dingus
Gizmo

Junk in the front

Not afraid to pun(t)

A fan of Paul Bunyan

His **Car** is his **THUNDER CHARIOT**
pushing 300 horses

3.6-liter V6 engine, which is rated at 299 hp and 666 pound-feet of torque.

*and/ or Butch/Dykes

51

Good Grief, More What If? (3)

(Choose the one that's the most you)

What If you took a wrong turn on the Ohio African Safari Tour and were surrounded by hungry lions?

A   I'd kick the rider off my motorcycle, gun it and jump the fence.

B   I'd take some raw meat out of my saddle bags and throw it at the gate keeper as I flew out.

C   I'd whip out my phone, point it at them and seduce them by narrating a Nature Film about these Noble Beasts.

D   I'd sing a chorus of *"Nice Kitty"* and have the lions join in with a dancing chorus line.

E   I'd 'audition' them for the new TV Game Show—**"I Aint Lion"**.

What If you stopped in a ghost town and were suddenly surrounded by a horde of hungry zombies?

A   I'd take out my (patented) Zombie harmonica and play *St. James Infirmary Blues* and have a Zombie Jamboree.

B   I'd mess up my hair and groan, "Hey guys, I'm hungry too, where can we get some fresh brains at this time of night?

C   I'd whip out my iPhone and shoot an MTV Zombie dance show.

D   I'd pull out my pocket flame thrower and roast the close ones and throw them on the Bar BQ and serve them up on fried bread. Zombies on toast, yum.

E   I'd eat as many as I could catch and put the rest in the freezer for later.

What If you were driving your boss to his daughters wedding and you got lost?

A   I'd ask if it was really as important as he acted about it.

B   I'd offer to give him a 10 % discount on the charge for gas and transportation.

C   I'd say that it was just my way of giving a little bit of excitement to an otherwise pretty boring day.

D   I'd ask if he and his wife were ever really married.

E   I'd offer to give the bride a quicky honeymoon myself, no charge.

More 'Good Grief, More' What If? (4)

(Choose the one that's the most you)

What If you were driving across an old rickety bridge and it suddenly collapsed?

A I would make a quick call to my insurance agent and extend my coverage.

B I'd call Fox News and try to sell my story to make a nasty Redneck troll reality series.

C I'd strap on my scuba tank and search for sunken treasure.

D I'd call my lawyer and tell him to sue the bridge contractors, the state, the car dealer, and the restaurant that sold me lunch.

E As I was falling I would sketch out a book, a Magazine, a Movie of the Week, and that TV series I saw in the B line up there.

What If you dreamt you were riding a motorcycle thru the Capitol Rotunda and foreign secret agents were shooting at you?

A I'd grab Arnold Schwarzenegger and use him as a human shield until I could make a weapon out of a flagpole and a trash can lid.

B I'd call my buddies from Seal Team 6 and I would surround the attackers on all sides while the team distracted them with a hilarious acrobatic clown act.

C I'd grab a banner rope and swing out, crashing thru a window, then I'd crash back in and swing round and round the spies until they were rendered immobile and senseless.

D I'd tweet out a call for my personal secret agent team of Julie Chen, Peewee Herman and Loni Love and let them work their terrorizing tactics on the poor shooters.

E Using a chair, my belt and underwear elastic I'd fashion a sling shot and shoot pens that would jam their firing pins and disarm them. I'd DEESTROY THEM. Hey, this is my dream, I can do whatever I want.

Driving a car is like Marrying a woman: you never know how far she'll go or what she can do until you get in her and start her up.

53

I am not the King of the Road
I am the Prince of the Pavement because:
My car is paid for.
My car is almost paid for.
My car is nearly almost paid for.
My car is partially paid for.
My car is nearly partially paid for.
My car is almost nearly partially paid for.
My car is Ready.
My car is ready for its first payment.
So many things have blocked me from making this
   first important payment.
I wonder if I might entreat you to grant me a
small loan that I might make my first payment.
I shall pay it all back on the first of the month.
I am sure I will have most of the money to pay you
   back on the first of the month.
At least half.
If not the first, definitely by the middle of the
   month.
Next month by the latest.
Then all I need to do is get my driver's license.
I'm already studying for my drivers exam.
Well, not studying quite yet, I can't study till I get
   my study guide.
That will be in the mail soon.   Very soon.
As soon as I can send for it.
Do you have a stamp I can borrow?
                              And an envelope?

What you bad Dudes and Divas should drive in:

Alabama—A Dixie-Mobil.
Alaska—A dog sled pulling a Polar bear on skis.
Arizona—A Firetruck to put out the Phoenix.
Arkansas—A Little Rock(et).
American Samoa—A Pago Pogo stick.
Brooklyn—A souped up bike.
Canada—A Caribou sled and a cold Caleche.
California—Stretch limos, Surf boards & broads.
Colorado—RVs & Skis.
Connecticut—The Dub-ya Bushmobil.
Delaware—A Mini Tricycle.
Florida—Porpoises, Water-skis and rockets.
Georgia—A Peanut GoCart(er).
Hawaii—Dugouts, Leis & Dune Buggies.
Idaho—A Potato-skin-burning Flivver.
Illinois—Conestoga wagon.
Indiana—A Dodge Cherokee.
Iowa—A Corn-burning Jalopy.
Kansas—Ruby Slippers.
Los Angeles—A Super Cruiser.
Kaintucky—A Thoroughbred and Sulky.
Louisiana-A Horse drawn chariot with a red stick.
Maine—Floatplane.
Massachusetts—A pony.
Michigan—Lake Schooner.
Minnesota—A Viking Longship.
Mississippi—A raft.
Missouri—Covered wagon.
Montana—Saddle up an Elk.
Maryland—A Navy Patrol boat.

Mexico—A Peon-driven Taxi with 30 riders.
Nebraska—A Lincoln MKX.
Nevada—See Vegas.
New England—A Double Decker Bus.
New Hampshire—Gerbil-Powered Mini.
New Joisey—A Repainted Hearse.
New Mexico—Acme jet skates—Meep meep.
Noo Yawk—A fleet of Limos and Garbage Trucks.
New Orleans—A Pony buggy.
N. Carolina—Tobacco Truck.
N Dakota—A MooseMobil.
Ohio—Junkers and Tow-trucks.
Oklahoma—Surrey with a fringe on top.
Oregon—Autosled.
Pennsylvania—Coal Truck.
Rhode Island—Jet Skates.
San Francisco-Rickshas, Trolleys and Gays, oh my.
S.Carolina—Golf Carts.
S.Dakota—Black Hills Presidential Limo (Stoned).
Tennessee—A Whiskey. A historical carrier.
TEXAS—An Austin Healey doing wheelies.
Utah—A Salt Wagon.
Vermont—A Snowplow.
Vegas—A Circus Calliope.
Virginia—Presidents baby pram.
Virgin Islands—Comes with a Frigate full of Seamen.
Washington-state Ghost Rider.
Wash. D.C.—Fertilizer Carryall.
Wisconsin—Milk Truck.
Wyoming—Buckboard.

I Dreamt I was the
Baddest Driver in the World:

I added JETO assist rockets to my VW so I could
   jump over traffic jams.

I mounted an airport Searchlight on the roof of my
   car for drivers that don't dim their lights.

I mounted flame throwers on my front fenders-buses
   & trucks move aside when I fire them up.

I reinforced all I my fenders so I can play bumper
   cars. Yeehaw!

I fixed the plow on my truck so I can push slow cars
   blocking me off the road.

It cost $10,000 but I can tap into the traffic grid
   and never get a red light.

Any cop about to stop me for speeding: I can tap his
   radio and send him on a call the other way.

Travelers Hint:
Go into a truck stop and chat up all the drivers till you
find one going your way. Hook onto them with a chain or
electromagnet and get a free ride to your destination.

Hurry Up Harry Says:

I have so many gas-saving devices on my engine
that I have to stop every hundred miles and
drain the extra gas out of my tank. If I don't
want to do that I can just drive backwards and
watch the gas level go back down. *You know—
negative entropy.*

It's just not fair :

~that you can drive on the roads and alleys but not
  on the sidewalks or rails.

~that you can run down deer and cats and cows
but not hikers or nuns.

~that it's okay to cut down trees but not okay to cut
down mailboxes and telephone poles.

~that cops can shoot at you but you're not allowed
to shoot at them.

~that you have to go to Med school to do brain surgery.

~that Kryptonite can kill Superman but not Spiderman.

~that you can't run down people that get in your way.

~that they don't make toasters big enuf for people.

~that armor piercing ammunition is not cheaper.

~that werewolves and vampires aren't real.

~that driving is not a full contact sport.

~that lawyers get paid to lie.

~that torture is illegal.

I Have the Right of Way because:

Yeehaw!
I am a VIP.
I stole this car.
This is not a Rental.
This is my ex-boyfriends car.
My mom taught me how to drive.
I am the office whiz on the percolator.
My Dad doesn't know I borrowed his keys.
I use much more expensive gas than you.
My GPS is way smarter than yours.
My auto is bigger than your car.
My fingernails need to dry.
I make more than you do.
My gal friend's preggo.
My ashtray's on fire.
I've been drinking.
I need a drink.
One Word:
PMS.
(Kinda unusual for a guy.)

What's your claim to Fame?
My scooter can go up steps.
My van can sleep thirty two.
My bus can bend in the middle.
My RV has a hot tub and a pool.
My minivan can go up escalators.
My truck can push 3 cars out of its way.
My Taxi has a live feed from the back seat.

The Top 10 Reason Why I get Tickets:

10   The police always pick on me.

9   Speed limits don't apply to me.

8   Maybe I should replace my **Screw the Fuzz** sticker.

7   They keep sending numnutz cops out to stop me.

6   Cops got no sense of humor when you insult them.

5   I have a stuffed wolf mounted on the roof.

4   Maybe it's my POLICE sticker.

3   Get off my friggin case you lousy flatfoots."

2   They don't think it's funny when you moon them.

1   #!#&*@$#%^&@!!!!

The Top 10 Reasons Why She DOES NOT get Tickets:

10   She drives topless and just gets a 'Warning'.

9   She has a James Bond license plate flipper.

8   3 snarling Dobermans in the back seat.

7   She gives excellent 'Breathalyzer'.

6   She works at a doughnut shop.

5   She has 5 police in her family.

4   Revved up afterburners.

3   Enticing Cleavage.

2   Connections.

1   $$$$$

Do not park beside any short red bald guys with no arms or you will get a ticket.

How to Gain Entrance to the Bad Driver's Guild

Hall of ~~Fame~~ Shame

These are the things you can do to get into the Hall of Shame:

- ➢
- ➢Speed.
- ➢Crowd.
- ➢Tailgate.
- ➢Peel out.
- ➢Flip the bird.
- ➢Scare pedestrians.
- ➢Turn without signaling.
- ➢Use your horn for everything.
- ➢Don't let others into your lane.
- ➢Ignore speed limits and stop signs.
- ➢Hog the road, drive on the white line.
- ➢Use yelling, cursing and rude gestures.
- ➢Speed up when someone is passing you.
- ➢Drink and drive and/or drive and drink.
- ➢Drive and text and/or text and drive.
- ➢Expect your car to repair itself.
- ➢Park illegally blocking others.
- ➢Hit your brakes for no reason.
- ➢Don't replace worn wipers.
- ➢Multitask while driving.
- ➢Don't dim your brights.
- ➢Cut other drivers off.
- ➢Bully other drivers.
- ➢Forget safety.
- ➢Steal gas.
- ➢Weave.
- ➢Hog.

The 10 Best Reasons
I Have for Driving
in the Big City:

10 You can double park anywhere.

9 You can throw your garbage anywhere.

8 There are more big windows to crash into.

7 The police are more reasonable (corruptible).

6 Alleys are better for ambushing dorks.

5 There are dope dealers on every corner.

4 There are ho's on every other corner.

3 The city never sleeps and neither do the ho's or dealers.

2 It's easier to slip away when you damage someone else's vehicle.

1 There are more moving targets: Jaywalkers Jay Runners, Drunks, Meter Maids, Traffic, Cops, Peanut Vendors, Nuns and lots of cats.

Riding up on someone's bumper lets them know that your business is more important than theirs.

City Drivers Know:

Be courteous, kind and considerate—it distracts other drivers and makes them easier to outmaneuver.

It's usually considered more sporting to give pedestrians a running start.

55 mph is a good, safe reasonable speed in a 25mph zone.

In the event of an earthquake—anywhere you are may be considered a restroom facility.

Overdriving compensates for over-drinking.

Don't forget the Roses—take the time to stop and pee on them.

I wanted the fast lane—but I got the half fast lane.

If your brakes fail—use pedestrians to slow your forward momentum.

Always slow down at the scene of an accident so you don't miss anything.

You are a cork—Life is a corkscrew.

My GPS can beat your GPS.

More City Driving Rulz and Sayingz

If you're driving your own car you have the right-of-way.

Keep your eyes on the road—if there's nothing interesting on the TV.

Kill the traffic computers before they take away our cars.

At one time I achieved complete harmonious integration with my car and the universe but then I sobered up.

If I told you what the secret of LIFE is—would you tell me where the restrooms are?

Think of Life as a connection between two levels of non-existence.

Think of Life as a big blue maze—and death as Pac man.

There are 8,000,000 stories in the Naked City—I'm a dozen of them.

You have two choices at all times—Life is the harder one, but its infinitely more interesting.

Never blame on the devil what has leaked out of your own warped cranium.

Meet me on the boulevard of broken screams.

I can drive faster—can you stop faster?

Passing me would be a Grave Error.

Jogging is not healthful—if you do it on my street.

No one respects a driver that always signals what he's going to do.

If God didn't want us to litter—He wouldn't have given us streets.

A responsible driver will swerve out of his way to teach a jaywalker a lesson.

To save time—avoid stop signs.

*End of Sequence—*HAPPY ~~MURDER~~ MOTORING

Another Self-Scoring
Bad Driver Test

When someone cuts in front of you—do you:
A   Wish them a good fulfilling day?
B   Curse them under your breath and smile?
C   Flip them the bird?
D   Blast them with your horn?
E   Follow them home and break their windows?
F   Run them off the road, shoot their dog and burn their bushes?

When you see a hitchhiker do you:
A   Wave?
B   Let them drive?
C   Swerve to scare them?
D   Swerve to bump them?
E   Flatten them and steal their suitcase?

When there's a traffic jam—do you:
A   Call somebody?
B   Yell at somebody?
C   Turn up the music?
D   Use your horn to clear the congestion?
E   Shoot at the cars in front of you?

What kind of driver R U? (are you?)
A   Polite, courteous, last in line.
B   Its MY car and MY road.
C   Accident on its way to happen.
D   Devil on wheels.
E   Have a ticket collection, pre jail-time.
F   On Dogs wanted list, Bad boys, bad boys, bad boys.

When you come to an intersection, who goes first?
A   All the other drivers.
B   The first to arrive.
C   Me!

Jeopardy

(Satire) All answers must be answered with a Question.

Answer: Possum Pudding with Starling Sauce.
Question: What's your favorite Road kill Recipe, Alex?

Answer: The biggest meanest vehicle.
Question: Who goes first at an intersection, Alex?

Answer: Grasshoppers, bunnies, raccoons and hitch-hikers.
Question: What do you scrape off your bumper, Alex?

Answer: Anything over 80.
Question: What's a safe speed on the Interstate, Alex?

Answer: I hope so.
Question: Does a bear crap in the woods?

Answer: A credit card or a gun.
Question: How do you pay for your gas?

Answer: Chelsea Handler.
Question: Who knows what evil lurks in the hearts of men?

Answer: Lindsay Lohan.
Question: Who is the Bad Driver's Handbook pinup girl?

Answer: The horn or suicide.
Question: What is the quickest way out of gridlock?

Answer: The Virgin, Buddha, and Garfield.
Question: Who are the patron saints of dashboards?

Jeopardy, too

Answer : A for overpass, F for underpass.
Question: What grades do you need to pass this Test?

Answer: Driving your Dads car home late.
Question: When can a car attain the speed of sound?

Answer: Gambling or suicide.
Question: What do you call drinking and driving?

Answer: A mother blanking garfarbly puckanosis.
Question: What do you call someone who cuts in front of you and slows down?

Answer: #@$%&#+@##!!!!
Question: What do you call someone who cuts you off?

Answer: How many you got?
Question: How many cops does it take to catch you?

Answer: A hot tub filled with Jell-O.
Question: What's making your van shake like that?

Answer: Would you mind kissing my butt?
Question: Would you mind opening your trunk, sir?

Answer: A load of doughnuts for Station Five.
Question: What's the rush, sir?

Answer: On the Road again.
Question: Why are you driving thru this field-where are you trying to go?

Answer: Will it never end?
Question: How long do you think this stupid game will go on?

We interrupt this program to bring you an urgent message from the author: If you haven't bought this book yet, what are you waiting for? If you have bought this book—our super grateful THANKS!!! We love you. We honor you. We wish you all the success in the world. Live long and prosper. Be happy. Go amidst the throngs of humanity and let them sing songs of praise to you. May the prophets smile upon you. Drive well.

We now return you to our regular programming:

Bad Driver's Handbook Quiz

Oh no not another dumb quiz . . . .
Wait, wait, this is no ordinary quiz—this quiz iz veddy special: uh . . . it has verbs and nouns and adverbs and all kinda stuff like dat.

INTRODUCING
The Fast and Furious Quiz

*If you are driving a car while you are taking this quiz—**are you out of your mind**? Stop the car or the bike or truck or treadmill and pull over and then take the quiz. We are not responsible for anyone that does not take all the normal precautions necessary when taking a quiz of this caliber. So there.*
Ready? Get set . . . . GO!

The safest driving speed is:
A 20 mph under the speed limit.
B The posted speed limit.
C 20 mph over the posted speed.
D Double the posted speed.
E There are no limits to how fast I can go.

You can warn other drivers about a speed trap by:
A Waving and pointing.
B Throwing a bottle at them.
C Beeping your horn in Morse code.
D Swerving towards them and screaming.
E Pulling along beside them and rapping on their windows.

You didn't think we would have that big stinkin' introduction to the Furious Quiz

and only have two entries did you—this farce continues on the next page and who knows where it will go from there.
What did we tell you—this is more of

The Fast and Furious Quiz.

All right—does anyone have to go to the lavatory?
Too bad. The Quiz goes NOW.

When is it safe to pass?

A   Never.
B   When the road is clear, the weather is good, yada, yada etc.
C   When I am late.
D   When I feel like it.
E   Anytime there are no other vehicles on the road.
F   After a few drinks, I AM the road.
G   If there are no elephants on the road.
     (This may be a trick question.)

What do you do if a policeman stops you and asks for help?

A   Gun it.
B   Laugh and hand him a doobie.
C   Ask for *his* license and registration.
D   Grab his keys and throw them in the weeds.
E   Ask how much money he has on him.
F.   Ask if you can play with his gun.

What do you do if a trucker plays chicken with you?

A   Tell his bartender.
B   Put a big FAIL on all his papers.
C   Hide one of his tires.
D   Disconnect his brake lines.
E   Get his wife, girlfriend and daughter pregnant.
F   Get his mother, mother-in-law and dog pregnant.

What do you do when an Amish kid gives you the finger?

A Shun him.

B Hide his prayerbook.

C Sabotage his butter churn.

D Tell his favorite sheep lies about him.

E Give him a Mohawk.

F Hide his silo.

My scooter is better than yours because:

A Mine is prettier.

B I can go 40mph.

C I have the papers for it.

D My skooter is hand painted and signed.

E I have high powered alkaline batteries in mine.

F I have completed two Tokyo Runs.

When challenged to 'lay rubber' I will:

A Throw down my condoms.

B Start my motor and prep my afterburners.

C Take out a loan on my house and bet it all.

D Put on my 'Wild One' cap and my James Dean jacket and stand
   with my legs apart and my silhouette back-lighted.

E Kiss my girl for luck, put my rabbits foot on my key—chain,
   hop on my moped and spin out.

**You hit some black ice and your vehicle turns
round and round and round:**

A I call my insurance agent and upgrade before I stop turning.

B I grab my guardian angel and we waltz down the highway.

C I just keep driving but I pull in at a rest-stop to change my
   undies.

D I scream, stop the car, throw up and text everyone what's what.

E I gain control, kiss St Christopher and drive off into the sunset.

A tree falls across the road blocking your way:

A   I jump out, karate chop the wood into kindling and sell it to some passing gypsies.

B   I whip out a chain saw from the glove compartment, cut the tree into Lincoln Logs and build a Roadside Rest.

C   I ram the tree out of the way with my car, then go get a new headlight and grill.

D   I call to my forest friends and we push the tree aside together. *(A bear came out of the woods and wiped his butt with a bunny but we all cooperated and moved the timber as a team.)*

I Tricked the PA Turnpike Toll-taker by:

A   Lying about my age.

B   Lying about the age of the girl with me.

C   Lying about how many girls were in the back seat.

D   Lying about how many cigarette cartons were in the trunk.

E   Saying it would kill my grandmother if I went to jail.

F   Photocopying a $100 bill.

G   Saying I was not gay.

H   Saying I was gay.

My Worst Bad Driving Trick was :

A   Making a hitch-hiker run after me three times.

B   Passing a whole line of cars waiting for an ambulance.

C   Giving a N.Y. Tourist bad directions to the Golden Gate Bridge. *(Go down 2 blocks & turn left, you can't miss it.)*

D   Herding elephants thru a Walmart.

E   Triple parking on Broadway.

F   Side swiping an Amish buggy.

G   Pushing a chauffeured limo into an illegal space.

Bad Drivers DICKionary

Daffynitions: so you know what you're yelling at other drivers

A Hole—asshole, anus:one who gives others shit.

Beaver—A small furry beast much loved by men.

BJ—Blow job, (who's Job?).

Boink—Boff, bang, screw, poke, nail, etc.

Cun't—Past participle of can't.

Cock—Rooster, gun action.

Cojones—Juevos.

Dipshit—Moron.

Doobie—Mary Jane.

Douchebag—A douche catchall.

Family Jewels—Family jewels.

Flagellation—Like waving a flag.

Flippin the Bird-Giving the finger.

Fuzz—Light prepubescent hair, pejorative term for policemen. *Well it's better than oinker.*

Gang Bang—Synchronized Fireworks.

Ho—Merry greeting.

Holden—Nads.

Horny—Hungry for sex.

Juevos—Hoden.

Junk—Package.

Mary Jane—Weed.

MILF—Make It Last Forever? Man I Love Friggin? Mom, I love you?

Muff diving-What better exercise for seamen?

Nads—Cojones.

Nookie—Like a cookie, only saltier.

Package—Junk.

Poo—An exclamation.

Poop—An elimination.

Poontang—50's quim.

Prick—To pierce slightly.

Pun—A malodorous misalign—ment of word meanings.

Pussy—An adorable loving critter, Without balls.

Queef—Vaginal fart.

Shag—*Brit.* Something to do with carpets.

Shit—Fecal matter, any odorous unwanted refuse, has a 1,000 different meanings, needs its own dickionary.

Slut—Very cheap prostitute.

Talleywhacker—like a penis, only bigger.

Tain't—Twixt sex organ & anus, tain't neither.

Titz—German teats, hooters.

Wanker—Self shagger.

Weed—420.

Whore—Short for Ho.

WTF—What The Heck?

420—Doobie

72—Magical page number.

Don't

DON'T DO WHEELIES ON BLACK ICE.

DON'T CALL A HARLEY A PUSSY BIKE.

DON'T FLIP OFF A TRUCKER THAT HAS A GATOR FOR A PET.

DON'T PASS ON A BLIND CURVE IN A SNOW STORM WHILE TEXTING AND DRINKING A RUM TODDY.

DON'T TRY TO MUSCLE AN 18 WHEELER OUT OF YOUR WAY UNLESS YOU'RE A 24 WHEELER.

DON'T WEAR GANG COLORS WHEN YOU'RE PUSHING YOUR SCOOTER THRU ANOTHER GANG'S TERRITORY.

DON'T COMPLAIN ABOUT THE LACK OF POLICE PROTECTION WHEN FLASHING A WAD IN A DIVE.

DON'T PICK A FIGHT WITH A ONE-EYED MUSCLE BOUND BARTENDER IN A SAILOR'S BAR.

DON'T TRY TO PASS OFF COUNTERFEITS IN A US TREASURY HOUSE.

DON'T DRIVE YOUR 'WHITE POWER' VAN THRU THE GHETTO PLAYING WAGNER.

DON'T DRIVE YOUR 'BLACK POWER' VAN THRU A NAZI-/-KKK RALLY PLAYING RAP CRAP.

DON'T DRIVE YOUR 'ABORIGINES GO HOME' VAN IN ADELAIDE PLAYING 'GOD SAVE THE QUEEN'.

DON'T TRY TO PUSH A HUMVEE OUT OF YOUR WAY-THEY MIGHT BACK UP OVER YOU.

DON'T THROW YOUR EMPTY BEER CANS AT COP CARS-THEY'RE SIMPLY FUSSY AND SENSITIVE ABOUT DENTS, SCRATCHES, AND KEYINGS.

DON'T YELL INSULTS AT A BIKER NAMED 'KILLER' WITH SWASTIKAS CARVED IN HIS CHEEKS AND CARRYING A RAPID FIRE WEAPON, DRINKING HOOCH FROM A KEG, KICKING A DOBERMAN, MAKING LOVE TO HIS GIRL NAMED 'BRUNO', AND WITH TATTOOS ALL OVER HIS BODY SAYING 'I DESTROY PEOPLE FOR A LIVING'. NUFF SAID.

DON'T STAY AT A MOTEL CALLED 'MOTHER'S PLACE.'

DON'T HITCHHIKE CARRYING A BOWLING BALL.

DON'T CHALLENGE BLACK AND WHITES TO A DRAG RACE, THEY'LL CHEAT.

DON'T RESPECT DRIVING LAWS IN OTHER LANDS UNLESS THEY RESPECT OURS.

DON'T RESPECT DRIVERS IN OTHER LANDS UNLESS THEY RESPECT YOU.

DON'T ASK BIKERS FOR DIRECTIONS WHEN THEY ARE HARASSING THE POLICE.

DON'T MAKE FUN OF BIKERS WHEN THEY ARE IN THE MIDDLE OF A "BUSINESS TRANSACTION.'

DON'T BOTHER BIKERS WHEN THEY ARE IN THE MIDST OF A GUN FIGHT.

DON'T LET THE TRASH IN YOUR CAR GET ABOVE EYE LEVEL.

DON'T DRINK ANYTHING LABELED 'HIGH OCTANE'.

DON'T PICK UP HITCHHIKERS WEARING A BALL AND CHAIN AND CARRYING A SAWED OFF SHOTGUN.

DON'T TRY TO BREAK UP A STREET GANG RUMBLE WITH A WHISTLE AND A BIBLE.

DON'T ASK A TRUCKER FOR A RECOMMENDATION WHILE HE'S IN A BARROOM BRAWL.

DON'T SWALLOW GRENADES WITH THE PIN PULLED.

DON'T GO TO A PAJAMA PARTY IN TRANSYLVANIA.

DON'T MAKE LOVE IN A BUSY INTERSECTION.

DON'T EAT ANYTHING IN A TV SET.

DON'T SLEEP IN THE FISHBOWL.

DON'T PLANT DUCKS.

DON'T STOP TO DELIBERATE WHEN SOMEONE ASKS IF YOU LOVE THEM.

HEY GANG, IT'S THE BAD IDEA FILE

Replace 'Punkin chunkin' with 'Junker chunkin'.
Toss them jalopies for their last ride.

Have Crash Test Dummies 'Crash' races: against a wall, off a cliff, etc..

Engineer a car shield like the Batmobile that covers your vehicle and prevents break ins.

Or better still, a device that gives a 12 volt shock to anyone that touches your car. *That'll stop those damn dogs and bitches that pee on our tires.*

And a car taser that shoots out a line and gives a jolt to that old geezer in front of you that just keeps creeping along.

Get them 007 James Bond SFX guys to fix up your car with rockets. machine guns, a snorkel, wings and an ejection seat.

A laser under your rear bumper that allows you to zap the tires of any car chasing you.

A bikini blowup doll that helps you get a ride when you're hitchhiking.

Avoid congestion and traffic jams with the blinking red light accessory and the siren app.

GPS technology should be implemented to give speed traps, and location of cop cars and bad neighborhoods.

Silent Partner: allows you to target and shoot something without taking your hands off the wheel.

A car with a manual pedal transmission in case you run out of gas. *Jes like Fred Flintstone.*

New Windshield Projection Grids will eliminate boring driving: now watch your favorite tv shows and films while traveling; have your own 'in flight' movies; *watch "Bullitt" or "Fast & Furious" as you evade the police in a REAL car chase.*

B.D.H. New Concepts
in Bad Driving Machines

Highway Gobblers

Traffic reduction by ingestion
Predator Motors Inc.

Solar Power Scooter

Humvee Town Car
Suburban Joyrider

Wind Biker

I bin drivin' this hyar
vehickle for nigh on to 40 yars and
only had two fill ups.

Roadway Cleanup Recycler

Dog eat Dog Factory

Junker   Squisher   Smoother   Yeehaw!!
                 Stretcher   Sprayer

Hey Look, it's more What IF? 5

(The Wild Side) Choose the best Answer for you..

What If you are driving up the Grand Canyon and a wild cougar attacks your car?

A   You whip out your laser pointer and run the red dot down the road and the cat follows it and leaps off the road and learns how to fly.

B   You mesmerize the cougar with the windshield wipers and when it jumps on the car to attack, you use the hood release to flip it out over the edge.

C   You use your GPS and some military connections to have the cat blown away.

D   You let your pet Siamese/Maine Coon out of the back-seat and she flies thru the air and beheads the cougar.

E   You put on a screaming fright mask and lunge at the cougar and it leaves a trail of pee in the air as it leaps over your car and runs up a sheer cliff.

F   You turn up the radio volume on a heated political debate and the cat strangles itself with its own tail.

What If you are having a tailgate Jamboree at the Stadium and a bear wanders up?

A   You give him a beer and a burger and ask which team he's on.

B   You give him a sports cap and an opposing jersey and shave 'FAN' on his butt.

C   You give him $200 and send him out to scalp tickets for your crew.

D   You put a white hat and apron on him and let him sell your leftovers.

E   You fix him up with your Mother-in-Law.

What If your tires go off the edge of the pavement:

A Cry.   B Scream.   C Call my mother.   D Wet my pants.

E Cut the wheel sharply and pull back on the highway.

I'm no dummy.

Rude and Rotten Rulz of the Road

The longest journey begins with a screeching peelout.

Never let anyone pass you—even if you have to run them off the road.

If my headlights are too bright—the other drivers should shut their eyes.

It is my job to scare pokey drivers that hold up traffic.

If someone leaves their car double parked blocking traffic, a good citizen is obliged to push them off the side of the road.

When you are handicapped for time there are special parking spaces reserved just for you.

Saint Christopher is the Driver's pal but Saint Patrick is the patron saint of Boozers.

Never warn other drivers about speed traps—better they should get a ticket than you.

If someone is broken down on the side of the road they should get someone else to help them.

Hitch-hikers and joggers ruin the beauty and flow of the highway—they should be eliminated.

Why should Police, Ambulances, and Fire Trucks have the right of way—they're not any more important than me.

If you see the constabulary has someone else pulled over you may save them a ticket if you beep your horn, give the cop the finger and take off like hell.

Beware: if your car is half full of garbage the rats and roaches may get organized and steal it.

Rude and Rotten Rulz Too

If you don't like my driving you should stay off my road.

Don't follow Police cars around—it freaks them out.

Oh, wait: DO follow Police cars—it freaks them out.

Don't play bumper tag with motorcyclists—they have been known to carry weapons.

Don't blast your horn at truckers, they may be having a bad day and 'accidentally' crush you.

Don't pick up a hitch-hiker carrying an M14 and wearing a mask.

Do not try to sell videos of a burning house to the owner.

Don't buy a "lucky rabbits foot": it sure didn't help the rabbit any.

If you see an overturned vehicle with people crawling away from it—DO NOT STOP—it may be a trap.

If you see a car with a foreign license plate that is in trouble do not intrude; instead help by sending a letter to their embassy describing the situation.

You can help jaywalkers that are disobeying the traffic laws by crossing where they should not, learn proper behavior by clipping them.

Driving on the sidewalk is not condoned unless you are being chased by the police or crooks or making a movie.

The Triple A formerly said to put your hands on the wheel at 2 & 10. Now with the new technology, keep one hand on the Phone, the other on the iPad & GPS and your knees on the wheel at 5 & 7.

**I am the reigning Monarch of the Road—
outta my way!!**

The Return Again of **What If?**

(Pick your poison)

What If you are lost in Las Vegas and a wild eyed cougar comes up and starts pawing you?

A   You buy her a couple drinks and fix her up with the bellboy.

B   You complement her on her style and give her a fake phone number and lift her credit cards and identity.

C   You offer to move her Caddy to a safer spot and then steal it and sell it to some drifters.

D   You tie her shoelaces together and tip her into a trash can and tickle her toesies.

E   You borrow five bucks to go out and get smokes and promise to call her when you get back from your latest undercover secret mission.

F   You slip out of the trick handcuffs you let her put on you and rappel down the building on the drapes.

What If you are driving a stolen police car and you see flashing red lights behind you?

A   You put on your fake cop hat and wave them past.

B   You swerve off the highway, drive cross country into the river and swim away.

C   You drive into a carwash, open all the windows, slip out thru the suds and escape into the sewers.

D   You tape a grenade to your St. Christopher statuette and pitch it thru the Constables windshield.

E   You drive into a Mall, up the wide escalator and hide in a Refrigerator Store Safe Driving Display.

F   You put on your Rose-Colored glasses and everything is suddenly super cool.

What If there isn't enuf room for another What If ??

A Cry.   B Whine.   C Wet your pants.   D Burn this book-
and buy another one, of course.

WANTED

ALIVE

$5,000 REWARD
OFFERED

This offer expires on Apr. 1, 1895

Description	Current Record
Eyes – Two	**CENSORED**
Nose – One	Previous Record
Complexion – Yes	**BORN**

The **FBI** did not endorse this poster

The Donut Shoppe

DONUT throw bricks or beer cans at Patrol Cars, throw them at Mounted Police or Bicycle Bobbies who can't chase you.

DONUT run into trucks, your airbag may blow your butt off.

DONUT drive to the ends of the earth. (Death Valley) "Here there be (dead) Dragonflies."

DONUT drive on ice covered rivers unless you have insulated underwear and webbed feet.

DONUT drive down ski jumps without your poles.

DONUT let your dog stick his head out the window without his goggles.

DONUT cover your car with rose petals without fertilizer.

DONUT ask for a trade-in on a car you drove thru the car dealerships plate glass window.

DONUT glide your Zamboni thru the Mall on Black Friday.

DONUT let your unicorn eat lasagna at Winkys.

DONUT forget the red carpet when the Kardassians stop at your garage.

DONUT perform an exorcism in your pajamas. (How the Devil got in my PJs I'll never know.)

DONUT push your luck with your transmission—change the oil every 10 years whether it needs it or not.

DONUT leave a 'tip' for your new girlfriend after a hot date.

DONUT look both ways at intersections if you're only going one way. DONUT change partners in mid screw.

DONUT wear plaid camouflage briefs with spats.

DONUT wash your hair with WD40.

DONUT walk the plank with chum in your pockets.

DONUT think that being in a parade puts you in show biz.

DONUT jump over Niagara Falls in a souped up tractor.

DONUT eat bronze doughnuts while sightseeing.

DONUT look in the trunk, please, Officer.

DONUT goose elephants.

The **Viper** is Coming

Official State Bad Driver's Eye Chart

Y

O U

A Z Z

H O L E

W H O T O L D

Y O U Y O U C O U L D

D R I V E ? G O H O M E

A N D P R A C T I C E

O N Y O U R C O M P U T E R

O R B O R R O W A B I C Y C L E

Official State publication © 1946

The Revenge of What If? 7

(Driving off the ends of the earth supplement)

What If you have just driven over a cop's foot and knocked down his motorcycle—What do you do?

A Make a pass at him.

B Ask him if he wants a beer.

C Ask if you can play with his weapon.

D Take down his name, badge number and doughnut.

E Repeat whatever he says in pig Latin.

What If you have side swiped a State Troopers Patrol car. Do you:

A Ask for his insurance papers?

B Offer to fix the scratches with house paint?

C Offer to put a matching scratch on the other side?

D Give him a stolen attorneys card and a fake garage?

E Take your keys and scratch in a cool design to hide the damage?

What If you accidentally run down a traffic cop and drag him for a block. Do you:

A Apologize and ask him to please let go of your car?

B Scream at him for scaring your kids and grandmother?

C Scold him that he's done quite enough and use a wet cloth to polish where he was hanging on?

D Offer him a drink from your pocket flask and ask where the nearest bar is?

E Cuss him out for his torn and wrinkled uniform and offer him a good price on a replacement from your trunk?

F Insist that he should get a really good insurance policy because of his dangerous profession?

More or less Revenge of What If ₈

What If You had your car worked on and now it only goes in reverse **?**

A. You could mount the headlights facing back on the rear bumper, turn the seats around and GO!
B. You could back it off the Empire State Building and collect the insurance.
C. You could enter a Jalopy Derby and back into place. The other Wheel Jockeys would go crazy trying to get you to turn around.
D. You back into your mechanics garage, walk backwardto the cashier, grab your check, back away to your car and back out.
E. Click and Clack, the Tappet Brothers, tell you to back your car into Lake Erie.

What If You were a Bitchin Biker trapped in a Bath and Body Works, surrounded by a horde of cooing, mewing salesgirls squirting you with sweet musky perfumes and pawing your body. What would you do to escape?

A. You could call on your gang buddies to help you out but they would make a video of your predicament and it would go viral on YouTube.
B. You could snatch a dozen brassieres, make a slingshot and shoot yourself out thru the front window to land on your bike and escape.
C. You could rub vanishing cream all over your body and disappear but the girls could follow you by your scent.
D. You get the girls on their knees to pray and run across their heads to escape out the exit.
E. You could fart your way to freedom.

When the cops are chasing you—do not:

A. adhere to the speed limits or they'll catch you.

B. bear down a dead end street unless you can levitate.

C. call your girl friend to complain about her facebook page.

D. drive thru a mall: unless you have a permit.

E. ever try to hide along the road, the ticket patrol know and use all these places.

F. fire back at the cops tires, they might lose control and ram into *you*.

G. go thru a construction zone—you are liable to end up with a cement overcoat.

H. hold your hand out the window to dry your fingernail polish, the cops may shoot and chip your nails.

I. indicate a left turn and make a right turn, it's illegal.

J. just plow thru leaf piles—there may be a fire hydrant hiding in there.

K. kite across intersections against the light—that's only safe when it's done by stunt drivers.

L. let your car fill with saltwater and try to swim home.

M. make an effort to teach grandma how to drive.

N. neglect praying when steering with no hands.

O. over edit when making a list of things to do later.

P. pitch doughnuts out the windows to slow the police-they won't stop and they'll be pissed that you wasted 'their' goodies.

Q. quit—or they'll catch you.

R. run into things.

S. slow down.

T. text.

Our BDH Super Hero:
BAD MOTORIST

PROFILE + ACCOUTERMENTS

Personal GPS

Pet Raven

Double Horney

USB jack

#@$% Mouth

MeeP MeeP

Move along

Red Neck

Super Megaphone

Air Horn[ey]

Masterful Fist of Fury

Detour

Misleading Signs

Tool Belt

Keys, lockpick, jimmy, crowbar, toll booth slugs, fake ID, handcuffs Solar Flashlite cutting torch Duct Tape

Bad Driver's Insult Book

Bladder catch bag

Jumper Cables

Sparky

B.M.s Sidekick Pooch

Siren

for cutting thru congestion

Fake Cop uniform

Extra Flair flares

Dino-Mite

for clearing road blocks

"Are we there yet ?" swatter

FUEL
Ethol
Diesel
Moonshine
Rocket
Plasma
Booze

The Big Finger Glove

Why I am Not in Jail:

◆ *I has connections.*

◆ *My misdeeds are not illegal.*

◆ *They haven't caught up with me.*

◆ *Bad Driving is not a criminal offense.*

◆ *My only witness is the dog and he aint talking.*

Was Ist Los ? (Huh?)

(A far out side bar)

You delve into the Supernatural and discover a talking car: What does it say?

A. It claims it was a professor of linguistics in Stuttgart and proudly transported der Fuhrer. You blow it to smithereens. Sieg Heil!

B. It claims its actually a robot from a robot planet trying to stop evil robots from destroying earth. You send it to a car psychiatrist.

C. The rusty, dirty old wreck spits a hawker of tobaccy and tells you to "get er done."

D. It says, "Call me 'Kit' and says it had a real hassle driving on beaches looking for a fuzz headed German singer.

E. Sam and Dean think their black '67 Chevy Impala is possessed by a dork angel{Castiel} so they call on SG-1s Helen [Naomi] Magnus (Amanda Tapping) to shoot it with the Winchester COLT (not a horse), it explodes in a Super gigantic FX Anime **Big Bang!**

Bad Driver Performance Evaluation

(15 of 15) **Excellent** *Far Exceeds* *Requirements*	(10 of 15) **Good** *Meets* *Requirements*	(5 of 15) **Fair** *Needs* *Improvement*	(1 of 15) **Unsatisfactory** *Fail* *FAIL*
Leaps tall build—ings in a single bound	Leaps short buildings	Runs into buildings	Crashes into buildings
Faster than a speeding bullet	Fast as a baseball	Fast as a horseshoe	Fast as a stalled car
Stronger than a locomotive	Stronger than a bulldozer	Shoots the bull	Smells like bull
Walks on water	Washes with water	Drinks water	Passes water
Talks with God	Talks with himself	Argues with himself	Loses these arguments
Designs computers	Builds computers	Runs computers	Runs from computers
Produces Films	Directs films	Writes films	Produces movies
Drives Superbly	Drives adequately	Drives poorly	RUN FOR YOUR LIFE!

Mumbles

Being another more exciting name for a miscellaneous

collection of stuff with no connecting theme except,

of course, Bad Drivers.

- Putting your arm out the window stabilizes the car and allows you to go faster.

- Smart drivers don't need turn signals because they know where *they're* going.

- Jogging is only healthful if you DON'T do it on my road.

- If the good Lord didn't want us to drive fast he wouldn't have given us ROADS.

- Keep your eyes on the road—if there's nothing interesting on the TV.

- If you bump a parked car in front of witnesses, get out and put a note on their windshield with a fake name and address: a really nice touch is scolding them for parking so poorly.

- You can tell if the emergency brake is engaged by the smoke.

- You can tell if the emergency brake is Engaged by the ring on its finger. (Sorry)

- Use your brakes as a last resort only if your horn fails.

- Yada, yada yada, blah, blah, blah.

Mumbles and More

- If God had wanted us to enjoy driving and sex he would have made everyone different.
- Practice steering with your knees in case you're with a lover who tells you to use both hands.
- I don't mind <u>hitting</u> pedestrians—I just don't want that crap all over my car.
- The shortest distance between two points is me in a moving car.
- It's easier to drive on ice and snow because you don't have to worry about stopping.
- The easiest signal for getting a slow driver out of the fast lane is a nudge.
- A low tire can be compensated for by driving sideways.
- Just kidding. A low tire can be compensated for by driving faster.
- Allow one car length stopping time for every 40 mph you are going.
- There is no reason for not running a car off the road that says, "I brake for teddy bears."
- Fast drivers are great at reaching hasty conclusions.

The train kept getting closer,
The Bad Driver ignored the bell,
The car went into the junk pile,
The Driver went screaming to hell.

Bumper Sticker Miscellanea

Personalized Nickname

Alien
Automaniac
BattyMobile
Blood Lust
Blood Sport
Butcher
Debt Mobile
Devil-may-care
Devil in a Blue Dress
Destructo
Grin Reaper
Hobo
Lawnmower Man
Liter of the Pack
The Borg Machine
Predator
Red Baron
Roaster
Road Hawk
Road Kill
Road Ravager
Speed Demon
Speed Kills
Terminator too
The Transporter
T, Rex of the Road
Velociraptor
Wild One

Random Bumper Ideas

Abandon Hope All Ye Who Enter Here
WARNING: Mad Driver
Comin' thru, sucka
Asphalt A-hole
Bars and S'Cars
Devil Driving Desperado
Driving Ms Crazy
Hotrod to Hell
I'd rather be Bald
Join the Sperm Liberation Movement
Idiot on Wheels
Impeach whatsisname
Jaywalkers: Beware!
Life in the Half Fast Zone
My Brain Eaten by Zombies
Ticket to Transylvania
Master of Tongue Fu
Mistress of the Dork
Moon over Mi-anus
Pussy with a Whip
Racing Rebel
Ride with the Reavers
The Road Commode
Sic Semper Tyrannis
Wanna ride on my 4Speed?
Zorro's Zoo

The Viper is coming

When you're screaming down the highway looking for a hard driving song that pulses with the beat of your motor, the nostalgic Willie Nelson's *On the Road Again* just doesn't cut it.

Here are some other choices:

Born to Be Wild—Steppenwolf
Back in Black—AC/DC
Bat Out of Hell—Meatloaf
Fast Car—Tracy Chapman
Highway to Hell—AC/DC
Highway 49—George Thorogood
Hit the Road, Jack—Percy Mayfield
Low Rider—War
Mercedes Benz—Janis Joplin
Mustang Sally—Wilson Pickett
Magic Carpet Ride—Steppenwolf
Running on Empty—Jackson Browne
Runnin' With the Devil—Van Halen
Shakin'—Eddie Money
Start Me Up—Rolling Stones
Already Gone—The Eagles

Okay you've burned off some calories, now lean back and enjoy the rest of the trip and the music.

I've Been Everywhere—Johnny Cash
Sweet Hitchhiker—Creedence Clearwater Revival
I Get Around—The Beach Boys
Ramblin' Man—The Allman Brothers
King of the Road—Roger Miller
I Can't Drive 55—Sammy Haggar
Drive My Car—The Beatles
Runnin' Down a Dream—Tom Petty
Free Bird—Lynyrd Skynyrd
Roadrunner—Bodiddley
Dead Skunk in the middle of the Road—Loudon Wainright

III

The Lyin' Cage

This is NOT the Liar's Page.

It never was the Liar's page.

There are no Lies on it.

This is not a lie.

That is not a lie.

We would never lie to you.

This is the last lie we'll ever tell.

See the previous page to find out how to collect your free $500.

We cannot ever tell a lie.

We never could tell a lie.

You really look GOOD today.

We never went to a parochial school so we know that nuns can never lie.

That's why we never lie. Never ever.

Now you can have your very own reality TV show—just send a wrapper from a Sniffles Candy bar to them.

You have won a brand new car in our secret raffle.

You have been chosen to ride as the Queen of the Night in the Wall Street parade.

A Nigerian bank has a check for a skillion dollars waiting for you.

You have been elected Chairman of the Board; everyone pays you $1,000.00.

They want to make a movie about your life.

This book/unit will explode in seven seconds unless you do exactly as I say_____

We absolutely refuse to have another

Lyin' Cage too

Let's not switch gears and not try something not completely not different.

Real Garage lies:

"If you don't get it fixed now you'll be sorry"
   (We'll be sorry too, we want your money.)

"The safest bet is to replace the whole thing."
   (The best bet for us. Well, moneywise.)

"We'll get you a new replacement"
   (If they start making them again.)

"They discontinued selling that screw by itself,
   now you have to buy a whole new unit."
      (Its just another one of our ways to screw you.)

"Looks like the last guy that worked on it
   didn't know what he was doing."
      (But I'm doing much better now.)

"We'll just get that total up on the computer,"
   (Joe, wake up and think of a number.)

"Either we fix it or you die on the highway.
   (Heaven forbid we lose another sucker.)

Would you believe—we don't have enuf space for another **Lyin' Cage** (3)

and this is not it!

Political lies we have learned to live with:

"I am not a crook."
President Nixon

"I did not have sexual relations with that woman."
President Clinton

"Well, there was no sex for 14 days."
--Ca Gov. Arnold Schwarzenegger

"They don't call me Tyrannosaurus Sex for nothing."
--Sen. Ted Kennedy

"No new taxes."
Pres. Bush Sr.

"Weapons of Mass Destruction . . ."
Pres Bush Jr

"If I don't have a woman every three days or so I get a terrible headache."
—Pres Kennedy

"Dan would rather play golf than have sex any day."
Marilyn Quayle, on Veep Quayle

"My fellow Americans, I'm pleased to announce that I've signed legislation out-lawing the Soviet Union. We begin bombing in five minutes."
Pres Ronald Reagan, joking during a mike check

We didn't have any more lyin' jokes left

so here they are not: **Lyin' Cage** (4)

Business Lies:
It's in the mail.   *(Almost.)*
We can't do that.   *(We're way too lazy.)*
It's never done that before.   *(It usually breaks.)*
No one else had any complaints about it.   *(Hah.)*
No <u>one</u> will lose their job with the new system/merger.
   (Every <u>one</u> will lose their job.)

Political Lies:
When I am elected-lies, lies, lies.
When I am re-elected-even more lies.
I promised the people . . .   *(Where's my dough?)*

Everyday lies:
It looks perfect on you.   *(They don't pay me enuf.)*
It's hardly noticeable.   *(If you keep your eyes shut.)*
We'll be back in a couple days to finish it up.
Honest Officer, I didn't yada, yada, yada.
Your Honor, we deeply respect the law and wouldn't do
   anything blah, blah, blah.
This is not the last lyin' page. Unless we're lying.

If a lie is the truth and the truth is a lie then are we not lying
when we don't say what we do not mean
unless it's Tuesday in Denmark?

Bad Driving Signs

Blood Donor Area

Mean Dog

DISTRACTION CROSSING

ROTC Crossing

HIGH DOPE AREA

THE POINT SYSTEM

Bad Driving Signs, too

Jet Crossing

Polluted Water

Jaws Crossing

Gay Werewolf
Area

Lovers Crossing

Bad Neighborhood

Toxic Waste Site

Very Bad Neighborhood

Bar Crossing

Really Bad Area

Prevaricator's Cage (5?)

You may think that this is just another thinly disguised Lyin' Cage but it's not, no way. This is a completely new and different idea. Just ask Gramma. Gram wouldn't lie would she? Of course not. Herewith some more examples of twisting reality to suit the speaker:

You're in perfect shape.   *(For the shape you're in.)*

Oh Honey, you're the only girl I've ever made love to, and definitely the best.

I'm sorry, Babe, but I got an emergency out of town I had to go to and I didn't have time to call anybody . . .

(Do I know you?)

Don't tell the boss, I shouldn't do this but I'm gonna give you the special discount price, cause I like you.

This is your lucky day, I can give you 20% off on those items.   *(We'll just double up on the other ones.)*

Honest your honor. I've never had one drink in my life. *(I've never been able to stop at one drink.)*

They fixed that in all the newer models.

The boss is busy right now making a deposit with our major distributor.   *(He's taking a crap.)*

Once the integrator starts to go the whole engine is gonna go.   *(The integrator is mythical.)*

Joe just took it out for a test drive to make sure everything is working perfectly.   *(Hey Joe, go out and check to make damn sure there aren't any rubbers or beer cans in that vehicle you and the guys have been using for your hot dates.)*

The Dreaded Return of What If?

What If someone throws a hornet's nest into your vehicle?

A You write a long explicit letter to your congressman complaining about the decay of morals in society.

B You bring in a reporter to get the hornets side of the story.

C You hire the Pied Piper of Hamlin to coax them out into a blender. *(Producing a drink with real bite.)*

D You sell the vehicle to the Green Hornet TV show. *(Sadly the actor playing Kato, the chauffeur, is hospitalized.)*

What If you were driving a bus and you were being chased by a pack of ravenous velociraptors?

A I'd call Steven Spielberg for help.

B I'd change the front marquee to read, "Comin Thru."

C I'd stop the bus, open the door and ask the raptors if they had a legal bus pass and the proper change.

D I'd pass out questionnaires to the passengers asking for evaluations of the situation and suggestions for practical solutions to the present problem.

E I'd push out the passengers one by one to slow the raptors down.

F Unless the Raptors were on Harleys I'd leave them in the dust. Yeehaw!

G I'd back up over them—the hell with 'science'.

H I'd pass out Uzis to the bus riders and offer a prize for the most kills.

What IF you are trapped between Grave-Digger and Megasaurus at a Monster Jam ?

A You call in the GhostBusters Stay Puft Marsh—mallow Man, the Jolly Green Giant and Godzilla and have a Battle to Extinction.

B You set off an *Acme* EMT bomb and it renders the electronic/mechanical vehicles powerless.

C You trigger a giant Hello Kitty® helium balloon and float up out of reach.

D You escape across the heads of the crowd in a mini-cycle you unfold from a secret place.

E You use your sonic screwdriver to reveal them as Daleks in disguise: you deactivate them and miniaturize them and pass them out to the crowd as souvenirs.

What If a Grizzly bear is in your camp trailer eating your couch?

A You ask him if he would like a hassock chaser.

B You shove a baseball bat up his butt and try to push the couch back out. C You go to *his* cave and pee on *his* rock pillow.

D You put your arm down his throat, grab his tail and pull him inside out and he goes running thru the woods naked and giggling, and tickled to death by his own fur.

E There is now a Grizzly bear rug in front of your fireplace.

This is definitely NOT the Prevaricator's Cage and we're pretty sure it's not the Liar's Cage . . . No, it's not BAD like them at all—we got tired of all those lies so this is not at all about people telling half truths and ridiculous exaggerations. Nope. This is

The Hole Truth

Catastrophe Lies:
No comment.
There is no danger.
Nothing has happened.
This is not an emergency situation.
The Emergency has been contained.
We were not notified of the danger.
The danger was exaggerated.
No one has died.
No one death can be directly connected to the accident.
There is no conclusive proof that the deaths and damage.
   are directly connected to the accident.
There was no emergency.
There was no danger.
Nothing happened.
No comment.

Company Lies
Don't worry.
There's nothing I can do.
I asked them and they said, "No."
You have nothing to worry about.
You'll get a raise in a few months.
This is your new 'assistant'.
Don't believe the rumors.
Don't worry.

Well, darn it, we are completely out of lies. Yep, don't have no more—and here they are **Hole Truth too** *From* the BDH *Great Lies Series:*

#5   I'll only take a minute.
#7   Its supposed to do that.
#9   I just love working here.
#13   I never even touched her.
#17   I was out with the girls. (F)
#19   I was out with the guys. (M)
#23   I have to work late tonight.
#27   I would *never* do anything like that.
#32   Sorry, there aren't any more *good* tables free.
#37   She must have me confused with someone else.
#39   We didn't know it was this bad when we made the estimate.
#42   Don't believe any lies in the paper about me.
#44   You must have done something wrong.
#47   It was so bad we had to replace it.
#66.6   The devil made me do it.
#67   It'll be ready Thursday.
#69   I'll just put the head in.
#100   I'll be out soon.

My favorite **lie** *rampage pours out of Jake Blues in* **The Blues Brothers** *movie when his ex-fiancée is about to* gun him down: **"Please don't kill us baby, it wasn't my fault, honest, I ran out of gas, I had a flat tire, I didn't have enough money for cab fare, my socks didn't come back from the cleaners, an old friend came in from out of town, someone stole my car, there was an earthquake, a terrible flood . . . It wasn't my fault, I swear to God!"** *He gives her the raised eyebrow, takes her in his arms and kisses her, she swoons and he drops her in the mud and takes off.* That's Lyin'!

Car Talk

Things you will hear said in an American vehicle.

Mooo. *(Lotsa people talk to cows.)*
I gotta go.
She started it.
What is that smell?
Mom! Make her stop.
Billys doing something.
What did that sign say?
I thought we had four kids.
We can't go back for it now.
Did you lock the back door?
Why is there smoke back there?
I can't remember if I turned it off.
Quick, hide the cans under the seat.
Sissy has to tell you something, Daddy.
Maybe we should stop and ask directions.
I hope we remembered to bring the directions to Grama's
    new apartment.
Really, shouldn't we tell them their tires are low?
Which kid wants to learn how to change a tire?
I think we should tell them they're on fire.
Please keep quiet and let me talk to him.
That lady doesn't have any clothes on.
Daddy, why are we stopping?
OMG I forgot my stash.
I know a short cut.
Who left one?
Owww!

BOOKS

Camping Out

Call of the Wild

GET OUT OF JAIL FREE CARDS

2,000 Leaks under the Sea

Pinocchio

Clinton

Outta my Way
Rhoda Wrage

Tiny Trips with Minnie Cooper

Dummys Guide to Trannys

The Big Girls Popup Book

Suicide Street
Jay Walker

Poly Ticks

Poly= many
Ticks= blood suckers

Good Mouse Keeping

The Big Bang Book

Start your Engines

Books we ~~fear~~ feel you might read

More Car Talk More or Less

Wake up, we're here. Next time, I'll drive.

Well, eat it off the seat or throw it out the window.

If you two don't stop that I'm gonna stop the car and you two can walk home.

But Dad, that's two hundred miles.

We'll need some lunch money.

Give me the tickets so I'll have them when we go in.

I thought you had them.

Oh $#^%&! Keep your &%^$# eyes on the road.

Why does that damn trucker keep riding our bumper?

Wave your boob at him and see if he wrecks.

That's why he was following so close.

How could we get lost in the place where we grew up?

I promised my Dad I wouldn't let anyone else drive.

You did it in my friggin car?

We didn't do anything, honest, Dad.

So when you took my car you lent it to your boyfriend and he gave it to his sister who traded it to her lawyer for a legal fee and we have to go across the border to pick it up?

Ask that guy with the machete where we are.

No!

Zip it up, we're almost there.

Do not let them look in the trunk when we cross.

You don't think we're gonna stop when we're on a

roll . . . **What If?** Is baack! (11)

What If a robot got in your vehicle and started talking trash?

A   I'd give it a demonstration of my rocket ejection system.

B   I'd ask it if it could talk to my computer and make it get on that Internet thingy.

C   I'd drive it to an ATM and tell it to clean it out.

D   I'd tell it all my AI (Artificial Intelligence) jokes and ask it if it could do any Transformer tricks.

E   I'd ask it if it was on Twitter and tell it to go tweet itself.

F   I'd ask it if it had any screw loose relatives scrumming in the Borg clan.

G   I'd give it a recording of Data *(Brent Spiner)* singing Asimov's 3 Laws of Robotics.

H   I'd ask it which-was-the-best: The Original **Star Trek**, the **JJ Abrams version** OR **Star Wars** and watch it melt down and implode.

What If you were sealed in a brick wall with a cask of Amontillado?

A   First thing; I would drink the cask.

B   Then I could finally get some quiet time.

C   When hunger and lack of air killed my buzz I'd go to-

D   Being pissed and kick out bricks so I could breathe.

E   Then I'd go out and bring back another cask.

F   And I'd drink that one, too.

Would you believe it? Even another What If?

What if your tongue got caught in your sippee cup while you were speeding on the speedway?

A You could call your lover and explain that your tongue was all swollen up and it needs someone to cool it down.

B It would be the perfect time to sing along with your old Heavy Metal Rock tapes.

C Or call your in-laws to apologize for everything.

D You could give a streetside shoutout for someone that's good with tongues.

E Now with a swollen wet tongue would be the best time to clean the inside of the windshield.

F You could have some fun with the cops by asking directions and repeating everything they say.

What If your gas petal gets stuck and you accelerate to 150 mph?

A Drop the iPad and stop texting.

B If you're chewing gum—spit it out.

C It's now really okay to use the horn.

D Try to get some relaxing music on the stereo.

E Don't stick your arm out the window anymore.

F Call your religious person and dictate your Eulogy.

G Now would be a good time to see what the brakes can do.

Badguy's
Believe It or Don't!®

Clyde Fenster of Okrachokeabee Florida has a car in the shape of a CUBE. He found it in an auto compacting junkyard

Brewster McGonigle (82) has spent his life collecting gas stations. So far he has saved up one.

Jake Looney has a collection of **84 vehicles** but has never learned to drive any of them.

A **Turnip** that looks like **Abe Lincoln**

Squinto Higgins carves totem poles with his teeth!

Cal Lesterol invented a three wheel unicycle

111

DAFFYNITIONS
I really had to stretch on these

Auto-maniac—I don't understand the question.

Beta Test—Letting the customer PAY to test it.

Berm—My alternate road side route.

Big Fat Axle—There's one in every car.

Billboard—*Bill not happy—Bill bored.*

Car Dealer—Selling dreams and phantoms.

Chicago—What the heck is a 'toddling town'?

Curb Feelers—Kootchy kootchy koo.

DEAD END—What you have from sitting too long.

Dealer—Make sure the deck is not stacked against you.

Driver—A club whose face has little slope for hitting long from the tee.

Grid Lock—"Everybody . . . . back up!"

High Def—"Hi, Def. How ya doin?"

Highway Hypnosis—You are getting sleepy: Wake or die.

Horn—My handle on controlling the world.

Insurance—Paying money for others bad driving.

JayWalkers—Suicide seekers.

Lawyer—Any brief joke will fit here.

Lug Nuts—Carrying a load.

Parking Lot—escaped from Sodom, wife into salt.

Road Hog—A greedy swine hogging my road.

Road Kill—Redneck Deli Service.

Road Song—Music about road apples?

Slippery when Wet—Keep that salesguy dry.

Speed Bumps—They never make *me* go any faster.

STOP Sign—Why are there no GO signs?

SLOW—Sorry, that doesn't make any sense to me.

Tourist—A stranger in a strange land.

Traffic Jam—A spread that is not sweet.

Truck Stop—A place to get your battery recharged.

Turn Signal—Used to be done by hand, now it's a red light.

Vanity Plates—Nuff said.

Van—A mobile motel room.

The **Viper** is Coming

Bumper Snickers

I WANT SEX AND I WANT IT NOW

Hey you, get off my highway

Grope one another

I THINK YOU WOULD FIT IN MY TRUNK

The bossy bitch is back

You are either bulletproof or very stupid

I usta blame my parents; now I blame my kids

Your time is up, monkeybrains

TIME TRASHES ALL

NEVER LOOK BACK

I'M NOT DONE HAVING FUN YET

Late for an appointment with destiny

Thank you for not smoking unless you're on fire

De-light at de end of de tunnel

We service the best

Screw this company and the ho's they rode in on

"No," means 'Maybe'

WORKING WITHOUT A NET

Never pet a werewolf

Lust is never having to say you're not ready

Love me as I am: terrific

            NEVER SAY CAN'T—
                    MAKE EXCUSES—
                            RAVE AND RANT

The Stupid Quiz

1 On a 4 lane highway the bus in front of you is going 42 MPH. The stupid truck passing it is going 43 MPH. How long will it take?

A. 2 hours.   B. 2.5 hours.   C. Forever D.A, B & C

2 The stupid cop that stopped you for speeding is giving you a lecture. You see his patrol car is rolling away. Do you tell him?

A. No.   B. Yes, as soon as he finishes his lecture.

3 You were driving too close to a coal truck and it threw back a pebble that chipped your windshield. Do you:

A.   Try to run him off the road?

B.   Tweet the hell out of him?

C.   Cry.

D.   Get it fixed before it spreads.

4 The stupid price of gas goes up again. Do you:

A.   Sell your gas guzzler and buy skates?

B.   Write nasty letters to the gas co. CEOs?

C.   Ignore it?

5 There is a stupid rhino (!?) blocking the road. Do you:

A.   Snap a picture giving it a hug?

B.   Friend it on facebook?

C.   Hitch your car to it—GiddyUp!

D.   Take it out and mount the head on the grill.

6 You find a VW Bug stuck in the under-carriage of your 18 wheeler. Do you:

A.   Give it to the kids to play with?

B.   Make it into jewelry for your lover?

C.   Put it in your collection?

D.   Hang it on the rearview mirror with the dice.

Oh no, not more Stupid Quiz

7 Eighteen stupid people try to get into your taxi at once. Do you:

A. Raise the fare?

B. Put extra hand straps on the roof?

C. Drain out some body fluids so they fit?

D. Give them skateboards and bumper ropes?

8 Your stupid motorcycle goes over a hill and you find yourself riding it thru the air. Do you:

A. Pray and/or swear? (#$%^&)

B. Look for some soft pavement?

C. Flap your arms like crazy?

D. Switch on your jet pack.

9 You have seen an ad on TV warning that there are too many stupid drivers on the roads. What do you do?

A. Ignore them and they'll go away.

B. Write my stupid congressman.

C. Redefine stupid to mean amusing.

D. Look at the top cartoon on page 121.

10 The stupid back road you are on narrows into a trail, then to a rut, then a path that goes up a tree and into a knothole. Do you:

A. Make a nest?

B. Try to get a lease?

C. Leave a note saying you'll be back with exciting news?

D. Go in, look around and ask if you can sublet?

E. Strip off your duds and get ready to be knotty?

F. Do you find out its knot what you thot?

EXCUSES We love 'em

I was doing my yoga exercises and got stuck in my love seat.

I tried to put the cat out but it refuses to give up smoking.

The car won't start because the battery is in the lawn mower.

I was going to take Granny to court but she wasn't in her cage.

My Psychiatrist said the stars advise not going out today.

I always get more hairy when there's a full moon.

The cat chewed thru my twitter account.

I want to sing and dance not work and sweat.

I always get a 'chubby' when I'm in the back seat.

I think I've developed an allergy to rising gas prices.

A squirrel broke my antenna by humping it.

I just saw Grandpa's picture on a wanted poster.

Our pastor says it's time for Armageddon.

I fixed the locks on my doors and now I can't get out.

My hemorrhoids got stuck in my wicker seat.

I was surfing the net and got hit by a humongous wave.

The dog ate my homework teacher.

My picture started appearing on milk cartons.

When I got on the bus everyone else got off.

They told me I was rotating my crops in the wrong direction.

I tried to get on my motorcycle and it ran away.

Gas prices got so high I had to stop eating beans.

I talked to my lawyer and she said I was a 'good boy'.

We played 'Farmer in the Dell' and the computer took my wife.

Even more EXCUSES

Every time I try to get out of bed the dog drags me back in.

My Jell-O experiments have begun to bear fruit.

I've modified my tractor to pull teeth.

My uncle Selma is pregnant again.

Everyone should have a productive hobby, mine is sleeping.

The parrot wants to learn two more languages.

I think my car is having an affair.

I have no idea why the food in the fridge keeps disappearing.

I'll cut down on my carbohydrates if you get me a scissors.

I keep my head in the fridge when I have a headache.

My drug supplier got slammed in a Ponzi scheme.

I asked my pickup to help me and it drove off in a Huff.

My coordinated swimming failed: the pool was drained.

My goldfish is afraid of the dark.

I think my car has been having bad dreams.

I looked in my tool kit and all I found was a worn out lawyer.

I know this sounds stupid but I just drove thru a chicken coop.

"Was anyone hurt?"

No but there was a lot of clucking and cheeping and swearing.

"Swearing?"

The farmer was in the chicken coop.

Solving Driving Problems

When in doubt—pass.

You can compensate for over-drinking by over-driving.

Fitting in a smaller parking space is no problem since I installed sharpened reinforced fenders.

It's a waste of time swearing at other drivers if they can't hear you—get a bull horn.

If I wanted other people to pass me I wouldn't drive down the middle of the road.

If someone ahead of you is afraid to move into the traffic lane a little nudge will give them courage.

It takes supreme self-control to NOT run cars off the road that say, 'I voted for the sonuvabeech'.

Why drive on the left when it's easier to outmaneuver slow drivers on the right.

Why won't they sell gun mountings for cars, we have a right to protect ourselves.

If you think you're way out in front—it may just mean you're going the wrong way.

THE TOP TWELVE WAYS TO KNOW YOU'RE A BAD DRIVER

12 Insurance salesmen won't return your calls.

11 The latest gps tracking device is named after you.

10 There's a weekly office pool on your next wreck.

9 There are radio traffic alerts whenever you drive.

8 You are at the top of the Insurance companies black list.

7 Comics make jokes about your driving abilities.

6 Rookie cops have to spend a week following you around.

5 Your name comes up twice on the State bar exam.

4 Five auto repair dealers have named their kids after you.

3 The state vehicle safety code has a separate chapter on you.

2 Claim adjustors appraise your new car to "save time".

1 Dr Kevorkian refers people to you for carpooling.

The Dreaded Return of What If?

What If your ashtrays are full?

A. We'll rent a big crane to turn the vehicle upside—down and shake it out.

B. We'll sprinkle sugar and ants in the trays and get an anteater to suck it all out.

C. We'll design a blower system that will vent air thru the ashtrays at 60 mph.

D. We'll design nanobots to convert the ashes to nuclear packets and bury them in New Jersey.

E. We'll put the vehicle on the space station and let the vacuum of space suck it clean.

F. We'll go to Marvel Comics and get Stan Lee to design a SuperHero that cleans AshTrays.

G. Oh what the hell, it's so simple—we'll get a new car.

What If you were an EMT on an ambulance and there was a 700 lb woman on the fifth floor?

A. We'd carry her down but it would take three trips.

B. We'd test her fat folds for resilience to see if we could bounce her into the ambulance.

C. We'd roll her into the elevator, cut the cable and scoop her out at the bottom. (Ewww)

D. We'd lock her in her room for 3 months, come back and fold her flat and sail her out the window.

E. We could cover her with airbags and roll her down the stairs.

F. We'd get 6 elephants to hold a circus tent to catch her when she jumped.

G. We'd lift the ambulance to her window with two Huey Helicopters, roll her in and fly her to her yoga class.

Holy Jeez, another What If?
Where will it end?

What If some clown tries to turn around in a tunnel and gets stuck?

A   You can't burn the SOB out of the way cause then you couldn't breathe and you'd get soot all over your windshield. Wish we had some TNT.

B. If we can get 3 cars lined up side by side we can push it the whole way out of the tunnel.

C, We can set up a car transport trailer so the trapped cars can shoot up it and over the stuck car.

D. Rev your car up so fumes pour out of your exhaust: and then sell gas masks.

E. You pump the stuck car full of helium and the driver leads his floating car out on a string.

F. Someone gets out a Jaws of Life and someone else produces a cutting torch and pretty soon the blocking car is a line of trash on the side of the road.

What If they're shooting a Zombie movie that's blocking your way?

A   A zombie head will make a great hood ornament.

B. They need more extras but you might not like what they have to eat.

C. Granny wants to get out to pee but you're afraid she might get rounded up and carried off.

D. They're already dead and messed up so driving thru them won't hurt anything.

E. You consider driving straight thru at full speed but don't want to get zombie guts all over your new car.

F. You wait till the Director shouts, "Action!" and you give them action. Yeehaw!

If it wasn't for half the readers of this book- the other half would be all of them.

MATTOON

Multi-tasking is a bitch on the road

Do NOT drive and Text

Fill in the _____ Blanks

With whatever suits your fancy.

1 _____gas prices and _____the gas companies that
try to _____ us.

2 Honest Officer, my _____ got caught in my _____
and before I could _____, it _____.

3 I _____ my car more than I _____ my wife.

4 I'm sorry but we can no longer _____your _____.
We just got _____ of your _____.

5 If it's the _____ thing I do, I'm gonna _____ you.

6 This car needs a new _____ and a _____ and
a set of _____s. Its gonna _____ you.

7 The louder your _____ is, the _____your _____.

8 My _____ has _____ but I can still _____.

9 The best driver will _____ on a _____
and _____ _____ on _____.

10 The baddest driver will not _____ on a _____
and _____ ety _____ on _____.

11 You see your Honor, all my _____are _____.
So I just cannot _____ anything.

12 Say Honey. Can you _____ my _____?

13 Sure, how many _____s do you want?

14 How many can you _____?

15 Recalculating? Is that the only _____ you do?

16 The more _____ I drink, the more _____ I think.

17 Who knows what evil _____ in the _____ of
_____? The _____ knows.

18 Look, Up in the sky, It's a _____. It's a _____.
Nyah, it's only _____.

19 Yo Bro, did the #%^^& _____ get the ^$#@
_____ you wanted?

20 The _____ _____ tried to put his _____ into
her _____ _____ but it backfired.

21 My Fellow Americans, I want to _____ you and
_____ you and _____ the house you rode in on.

ROADRAGE :

1 Is its own reward.
2 Is our God given American right.
3 Should be carefully nurtured and praised.
4 Should be a justifiable defense in court.
5 Is Non-racist, non-sexist and non-vehicled.
6 And it crosses all economic lines.
7 It's the number 13 cause of divorces.
   (The # 1 cause is, of course, marriages.)
8 It contributes to our economy by selling more car
   replacement parts and filling junk yards.
9 And that doesn't include Aspirin, Tylenol, lawyer fees
   and kicked in fenders.
10 Is the number one pick of the National Psychiatric
   Association for supporting *the Yacht League.*

My Most Baddest Driving Tricks were:

A Chaining two 18 wheelers together end to end. You shoulda
   seen those two truckers trying to pull away.
B I've programmed the ATM at the truckers bar to send me any
   duplicate payments drunks make by mistake.
C I welded an air whistle to the top of a tanker cab—whenever
   they hit 60 mph a weird warbling whistle will come from
   nowhere.
D I laid out a shortcut detour up to a wall—and I painted a traffic
   tunnel on the wall. Wiley, huh?
E Did you ever make a stencil that says "WE SUCK" and spray it
   on the side of a cop car? Me Neither.
F I made a portable toll station on the back of my truck that I
   can set up at random bridges. (*The cops are mad as hell when
   they pay to get thru and check it out and come back and find its
   gone. I call it the Phriggin' Phantom Toll Booth.*)

If life is not fair—cheat

More Snickers

The longest drive begins when you find your keys

NEVER GIVE THE OTHER DRIVER AN EVEN BREAK
SORTA W. C. FIELDS

If you think Life isn't fair—
You're gonna hate death

Have no fear—speed demon is here

Bury my heart at the Indy 500

THESE SPEED BUMPS PLACED HERE FOR YOUR PROTECTION
by Ed's Chassis Alignment Center
We are Collusion experts

We are NOT lost—we are on an adventure

Omigawd—not deja vu again

Nurture your delusion

Dump the toxic wastes in the cities
where they belong

You're either in the fast lane or the half fast lane

*Life is vicious   Life is cruel
Unless you have
A lot of pull*

It's Their Fault:

If you're having trouble with your driving you gotta blame it on someone . . .

➤ THEY should make STOP signs easier to read.

➤ THEY shouldn't put so many stop signs in a row.

➤ THEY should not allow fog in these low lying areas.

➤ THEY should make telephone poles stronger than that.

➤ THEY shouldn't put mailboxes in the way of shortcuts.

➤ THEY should put fireplugs where they're not in the way.

➤ THEY shouldn't have breakable stuff so close to the road.

➤ THEY should have the road wide enough to make U-turns.

➤ THEY should put up signs that tell you when you're off the road.

➤ THEY should make roads smoother so they don't wake you up.

➤ THEY shouldn't have sharp curves so close to the hospital.

➤ THEY should put cow catchers on cars so it doesn't happen.

➤ THEY should put deer crossing signs where it's safer.

➤ TUNNELS shoud be short enough so you don't fall asleep.

➤ THEY should put up fences so you can't accidentally go thru all those yards.

THEY shouldn't let drivers like me on the road.

Top 10 Reasons
Why You Shouldn't Try to Cut Me Off

10 I'm armed.
9   My wife's armed.
8   My kids are armed.
7   My dog has a shotgun.
6   They're all pointed at you.
5   We have auto-targeted machine guns, TOO.
4   And a GPS guided laser that controls
3   A J-70 Jet-assisted target missile,
2   With 10 backup missiles.
1   Ready, Aim . . .

How to Get Out of a Ticket

A Cleavage.
B Cleavage and size.
C Cleavage, size and lipstick.
D Cleavage, size, lipstick and a smile.
E Cleavage, size, lipstick, and a BJ.
F A BJ.
G Silent weeping. *[Hysterical weeping won't work.]*
H Hysterical laughter with jiggling cleavage.
I A three letter license plate.
J Official police window stickers.
K Donut cartons for the Police Ball in the back seat.
L Share a doobie.

Anything the mind of man can invent — the mind of man can pervert.

I don't care what Spock says Mr Sulu, we're not going to Disneyland.

The Great BDH Tech Race

EGOPIE

Hi Yo Sliver. on and on trusty steed.

Whew

I smell gas.

Candy? Cigars? Mentos? iPads?

Some Final Quotes

The potholes are always smaller in the other lane.
Virginia Host

There are old racers and bald racers but there are no old bald racers that don't walk funny.
Harry Clark

You're in a river of excrement in a native American water vessel without a means of propulsion.
Sheldon Cooper (B.B.T) (C. Lorre)

Big trucks have the 'right of weight'.
Bubba Harris

We ran into a cat. When we went back to look at its collar it said the owner's name was Schrodinger. But then the cat jumped into a dumpster and we lost it so we didn't know what condition it was in: whether it was alive or dead.
Wolfe Eberhardt

I can't go to hell, Lucifer has a Restraining Order against me.
Bubba Harris

I have to drive fast so I can get there before I forget where I'm going.
Grandpa Jones

Retired doesn't mean I need new tires, it means I'm tired again.
Cleavon Smith

I caint retire—then I could never get a day off again.
Bubba Harris

And Ass orted Sayings

Aint drivin a bitch? *Socrates*

Turn signals give the other driver an unfair advantage.

Never take chances or drive crazy without your seat belt-
that's what it's for.

Smoking is like putting a squirrel in your mouth:
everything is okay until you light it on fire.
George Burns

**Smoking cancels out
drinking if you go fast enough.**

I be afflicted with that C.A.R.S. Disease: Can't Ardly Remember Shit
Grandpa Jones

There's a fine line between insanity and madness.
Dr Robert Goldsmith

Sex is no mystery anymore but women still are. *Mattoon*

When you're young there's always some old fart crawling
along in front of you holding you back.
When you're old and driving at a safe speed there's always
some punk kid behind you trying to push you outta the way.
The joke is it's the same person at different ages.

I have a running vehicle and a credit card-
I can go wherever I want, whenever I want and do what I want.

**There is no gas shortage in this book:
effervescence and flatulence at your service**

Of all the Bad, Bad Books you've looked at- this is the one you're looking at now!

I have an ice cube ready to drop down your back if you skip this one.

What If you're riding your camel thru Walmart and you are suddenly attacked by a gang of rabid penguins, what the hell do you do?

A. Give them all bowties, tap-shoes and dance lessons and put them on Dancing with the Stars.
B. Flood the Cold Storage Warehouse, give them skates and audition for Ice Capades of 2020 doing
Putting on the Ritz.
C. Lead them to the Penguin Section and push them down the Penguin slide into the Penguin shredder.
D. Feed them into the down slot of the up escalator. When they come out at the other end they are ironed out flat. You can sell them as decorations and capes at the Oscars.

What if someone in a Welcome Wagon throws a brick thru your window?

A. You blow up their clubhouse.
B. And you cut off their puta supply.
C. And you cut off their puto supply.
D. And you send a nasty letter to their Mamacita.
E. And you fix their wheels so they won't turn to the right.
F. And you register them as Republicans.
G. And you change their gang colors.

What If you rented a car and there was a naked lady tied up in the trunk?

A. I'd ask her if she was ticklish.
B. I'd ask her if she was into body painting.
C. I'd ask if she would like to star in a movie.
D. I'd ask her if she would mind taking a breathalyzer test.
E. I'd ask her if she would mind being first prize in the Policeman's Ball raffle.

Your diplomatic immunity plate
aint gonna help you here, boy.

No, no this is not a What If? Oh no this is an umm . . . . a King Kong Extra. Yeah, that's it.

What if King Kong escaped and was hiding in your bathroom?

A. I'd tell him to use the guest toothbrush or on second thought—the toilet brush.
B. I'd ask him if he wanted to go for a ride on my car.
C. I'd ask him if he was hungry and if he liked leather couches and beanbag chairs.
D. I'd call the plumber and tell him to get ready for a big surprise.
E. I'd order a shipload of toilet paper.

What If your Mother-in-law caught you in bed with a young cow?

A. I'd ask her if she would like some sex or some veal.
B. I'd ask her if she ever had a 3-way with a family member.
C. I'd ask her if she wanted to get involved in my new weight loss program.
D. I'd introduce her to the calf and determine what they had in common.
E. I'd ask her if she wanted to watch, join in or run the video camera.
F. I'd wink, give the calf a slap on the rump, and say, "Next."

Money back Guarantee:

If you purchase this book and we are not satisfied with your money we will give it back to one of the stripper's we owe money to.

Guarantee #2 If you are not completely convinced that we have warped the livin hell out of your mind : just return the unused portion of your brain and we will return the unused portion of your money.

Another even better Money Back Guarantee:

If you are not perfectly satisfied with this copy of the **Bad Drivers Handbook** please return it absolutely free with our compliments. Include in the return package a Money Order or check for $2.98 for postage and handling. Residents of foreign countries and Nebraska please include a postage stamp or International Postal reply Coupon worth $6.66.

All others enclose a self-addressed stamped envelope,five (5) separate stock certificates and a small gold bar weighing at least 14 ounces.

Purchasers west of the Allegheny River should enclose 100 Krugerrands for every vowel in your name. Others may send small unmarked bills equal in weight to their primary mode of transportation or domicile, whichever is more.

ExCons please supply an extra thirty thousand dollars for a surprise present for the author of this atrocity.

Immediately upon receipt of your missive we will begin to endeavor to start the procedure to locate your file.

Please allow 4 to 6 years for delivery of your replacement copy.

BAD DRIVER'S HANDBOOK

Introduction: Previously a punk driver in a 65 foot rig whipped around us and swerved and banged into us nearly knocking us off the Homestead high level bridge. My ladyfriend had a real heart attack. The young trucker didn't believe he did it because he was in a rush and didn't know what he was doing in a big rig. Bad attitude.

```
Deadication /I miss my driving
Companion, Rose.
```

If you're insulted or uncomfortable because you know people that read this book are laffing at you—Good.

If you are reading this while you are driving
Hoo boy do I put a CURSE on you.

Bad Driver's May Ignore these notes
Like more or less serious advice:

Following close behind big trucks will result in window stars when small rocks are spun back against your windshield. Stay back.

Other (Bad)drivers can't see you when coming around blind curves. Hug your side of the road so they can't crowd you and take you out. Stay right.

Pissed off motorcycle riders often carry metal marbles to throw back at your windshield if you follow too closely. Stay back.

BadDriversHandbook@AOL.com

Afterward:

If someone gives you this book, it's because they love you and don't want to see you destroy yourself or the people you love.

OR they are afraid to go out on the streets with you driving the way you do.

**Please Take Heed. Laff at these drivers,
but don't be them.**

For any bluenoses without a sense of humor that still don't get the point : I am NOT supporting Bad Drivers: I am satirizing them, savaging them, making fun of them so they wake up and stop taking lives.

Do you feel we might be making fun of your bad driving attitude?   We are.

Everybody, young and old, male and female THINKS they're a good driver: after they drive for a year. There are 5,767 driving accidents every day. 145 fatalities. That's like driving thru a city the size of Walden, N.Y. and EVERYONE in the city is in a wreck. Or driving down a highway and every 15 seconds you see a smashup, and every 12 minutes you pass a fatal crash.

Remember these images when you're driving.

You can't go back in time and **unwreck**
no matter how much you pray.

You can't undo it once it's done.

THE ONLY WAY TO
AVOID AN ACCIDENT IS **TO NOT HAVE IT**

BY DRIVING CAREFULLY **ALL THE TIME.**

You can't save *your* life if you're drinking.   *Hank*

THE BAD DRIVER'S QUESTIONNAIRE

In order to more fully understand who you are we ask you to take this little quiz about who you think you are. It shouldn't take more than a couple hours.

NAME.. Alias ....

Fake name you give at accidents ....

Fake name on your fake ID...

Name your Momma called you ....

Nickname you would like to be called...

Nickname you are actually called...

SuperHero Name...

ADDRESS ....

No kidding—you really live in a vacant lot? ....

Have you lived here less than 3 days? Yes........... No...........

Last known address...

Address where you actually pick up your mail ....

Address where you want your 10 million Dollars Publisher's Sweepstakes check delivered...

Address where, Dog the Bounty Hunter, can find you? ....

CELL PHONE NUMBER..

Last cell phone #........................... One before that ....

Disposable cell phone #................. Untraceable #.............................

Do you have a girl friend or boy friend? Yes...........No...........

Are they hot? Are they easy? Phone # ?...

Wife or husband or "friend"? Are they hot? ....

Are they easy? Phone? ....

Do you have a Mother? Address...

Would she pay a ransom over $10,000 for you? ....

Would you pay a ransom over $10,000 for her? ....

Is she easy? Is she hot? Her Phone? ....

YOUR AGE........... No, your real age...........

SEX Yes........... No...........

HOBBIES................................Other lame pastimes ....

NUMBER OF CRASHES THIS WEEK............... YESTERDAY ....

NUMBER OF TICKETS THIS WEEK?............... TODAY?.................

*You can make a copy of these 2 pages of this book to give to your relatives or friends to see if they could be helped by the **Bad Driver's Handbook.***

LAST WILL AND TESTAMENT ....
....
Who gets your Mercedes? ....
Who gets your iPad? ....
Who gets your Vibrator? ....
Who gets your Big Wheels? ....
Who gets your Ticket collection? ....
Who gets your GPS? ....
Who gets your Bad Drivers Handbook? ....
Who gets your naughty tapes? ....
DO YOU LIKE GLADIATOR MOVIES? Yes........... No...........
DO YOU LIKE BEACH BLANKET MOVIES? Yes........... No...........
DO YOU MISS NELLIE BLY? Yes........... No...........
DO YOU MISS SHEENA, QUEEN OF THE JUNGLE?
Yes...........No...........
DO YOU MISS XENA, WARRIOR PRINCESS? Yes........... No...........
WOULD YOU DATE LARA CROFT? Yes........... No...........
WOULD YOU DATE BRUCE CAMPBELL, THE CHIN?
Yes........... No...........
DO YOU LIKE MOVIES WITH NAKED ANIMALS? Yes....... No ....
DO YOU LIKE NAKED ANIMALS WITH MOVIES? Yes....... No ....
WOULD YOU HAVE A SMOKE WITH A FURRY? Yes....... No ....
HOW OFTEN DO YOU THINK SOMEONE SHOULD
BE WHIPPED?
HOW LONG WOULD YOU SWIM IN JELL-O? ....
EVER BEEN TO A DUNGEON? Yes....... No.......
DID YOU PAY THEM? Yes....... No....... DID THEY PAY YOU?
Yes......No.......
HAVE YOU EVER DONE IT ON A UNICYCLE? Yes....... No.......
DO YOU THINK BIG TRUCKS ARE ROMANTIC? Yes....... No.......
DO YOU BELIEVE IN CAPITAL PUNISHMENT? Yes....... No.......
WHICH CAPITAL DO YOU PREFER?.......
HAVE YOU EVER DATED A TV OR MOVIE STAR? Yes....... No...........
THEIR NAME ....
ARE THEY HOT? Yes....... No.......
THEIR PRIVATE PHONE #..
EVER DATED A POLITICIAN? Yes....... No.......
GOT ANY DIRT ON THEM? Yes....... No.......
WHAT'S IT WORTH? $ .... *NEED HELP COLLECTING?*
Yes......No.......
WHAT NATIONALITY ARE YOU?........... *WHAT SPECIES?*................

Thank you for filling out the BAD DRIVER QUESTIONNAIRE form. We will review your
answers and if we like them we'll get back to you.
Don't hold your breath . . .